Marvelous Minilessons for Teaching
Nonfiction Writing K-3

LORI JAMISON ROG

Pembroke Publishers Limited

This book is dedicated to the memory of PK,
who was always my biggest fan, as I was his.

© 2015 Lori Jamison Rog

Pembroke Publishers
538 Hood Road
Markham, Ontario, Canada L3R 3K9
www.pembrokepublishers.com

Distributed in the U.S. by Stenhouse Publishers
480 Congress Street
Portland, ME 04101
www.stenhouse.com

Library and Archives Canada Cataloguing in Publication

Rog, Lori Jamison, author
    Marvelous minilessons for teaching nonfiction writing K-3 / Lori Jamison Rog.

Includes bibliographical references and index.
Issued in print and electronic formats.
ISBN 978-1-55138-303-3 (paperback).--ISBN 978-1-55138-907-3 (pdf)

    1. English language--Composition and exercises--Study and teaching (Early childhood). 2. Report writing--Study and teaching (Early childhood). 3. Language arts (Early childhood). I. Title.

LB1139.5.L35R6365 2015   372.62'3   C2015-903642-9
                                         C2015-903643-7

Editors: Jane McNulty, Alison Parker
Cover Design: John Zehethofer
Typesetting: Jay Tee Graphics Ltd.

Printed and bound in Canada
9 8 7 6 5 4 3 2 1

Contents

Introduction

Welcome to the wonderful world of nonfiction for kids in primary grades!

Wait a minute.... Isn't pretty much *everything* beginning writers write non-fiction? As they embark on their literacy journey, our children tend to write almost exclusively about what they can do, or have done, or "lik" to do. In spite of the emphasis on *reading* narrative fiction in the early years, imaginative or fictional *writing* doesn't usually emerge until Grade 2 or 3. Furthermore, current educational trends, from inquiry-based learning to Common Core Standards, are demanding that even our youngest writers be able to convey information and even attend to audience, purpose, and genre in writing.

Too often, we've assumed that children will simply learn to write by writing. As a result, we fall into the trap of *assigning* more than *teaching*. We tell students to *write a report on an animal* or *write a poem about spring*. But what does that teach them about being better writers? Instead of focusing on the *product*—the report or the poem or the story—we need to attend to what it is that good writers *do*.

An extensive body of research suggests that teaching writing *strategies* is the single most effective way to improve student writing (Graham et al., 2012). Writing strategies may be described as the deliberate actions a writer does to make a piece of writing as clear, powerful, and effective as possible. Strategies may take the form of planning or revising routines, such as gathering facts or inserting details. They may involve composition, such as crafting leads that hook a reader's attention, using similes to make comparisons, or choosing verbs that energize writing. And sometimes they represent a strategic approach to conventions, such as analyzing where to put the apostrophe in a contraction or integrating semantic and syntactic clues when deciding how to spell an unfamiliar word.

There's no question that lower-level transcribing skills (letter formation, letter-sound connections, directionality, and spacing) are also critically important in the early years, as young writers learn to use marks on the page to represent the ideas in their heads. As it happens, we primary teachers are already pretty good at teaching these skills. In a survey of 300 Grades 1 to 3 teachers across the United States, Steve Graham and Laura Cutler reported that teachers were more likely to provide daily instruction in spelling, grammar, and punctuation than in any other aspect of writing (Graham & Cutler, 2008). One of Graham and Cutler's key recommendations is that primary teachers strive for a better balance of basic skills and writing strategies. Here's where this book can help. Each of the mini-lessons in this book focuses on teaching a specific strategy for planning, crafting, or revising student writing.

The Power of the Minilesson

The great thing about writing instruction is its simplicity. No special tools are needed, other than something to write with and something to write on. We show the students what writers do by modeling writing ourselves. And as we write, we think aloud; in other words, we articulate our reasoning as we decide what words to use or how to put those words together.

Interestingly, our shortest lessons may very well be our most effective ones. That's the philosophy behind the *minilesson*—a brief and intentional instructional routine that focuses on a specific learning goal or writing strategy. Here are seven things to remember in preparing and presenting effective minilessons:

- **One specific learning goal:** Target a writing strategy that focuses on what we want our writers to know or be able to do. It should be a strategy that students can transfer to other writing situations as well. Focus on only one goal at a time. A combination of your local curriculum standards/outcomes and your own ongoing assessments of your students will provide you with more lesson ideas than you'll ever have time to use!
- **A catchy title that students will be able to hang on to:** Make sure students know what it is they're learning, in language they'll be able to understand and apply. For example, in this book you'll find minilessons on "bossy sentences" (imperative sentence structures) and "bubblegum writing" (inventive spelling).
- **Brevity:** Remember that it's a minilesson, not a maxilesson! If necessary, set a timer for ten minutes and when the timer sounds, stop the lesson. You can always finish it another day.
- **Modeling:** The very best way to teach children what writers do is to show them. Model writing for the students, "thinking aloud" your own process of getting the words on the page (or screen). Sometimes you'll compose the text yourself, and sometimes you'll invite the students to collaborate in composing the text while you scribe, showing them what their words look like in print.
- **Guided practice:** Give the students a chance to try out the strategy in a safe and supportive setting, whether as a large-group "shared writing" experience, or in pairs or small groups.
- **Independent application:** Establish the expectation that students should incorporate what they learned in the minilesson into their own independent writing.
- **Repetition:** Don't expect that all your students will master a concept or strategy after one ten-minute minilesson. Repeating a lesson several times—with the whole class or with targeted small groups—will help to ensure that all your students develop the habits of highly effective writers.

As with every other course of learning, writing instruction should be guided by assessment of what our students know and can do. The learning goals we select and the lessons we teach will depend on the developmental stages and levels of sophistication of our students. Although every writer is different, most children go through a set of broad, fairly consistent stages on the journey from emergent to independent literacy, stages which are paralleled in reading and writing.

Stages on the Journey to Literacy

Primary teachers have always been under a lot of pressure to make sure their students learn to read. And admirable as this focus is, it has sometimes meant that other subjects such as writing have fallen by the wayside. In fact, writing has been referred to as "the neglected R" (The National Commission on Writing in America's Schools and Colleges, 2003).

But the good news is that when we focus on writing, our children also become better readers! At no stage of children's cognitive development are reading and writing as interconnected as they are during the primary grades. A chart summarizing these stages of reading and writing development may be found on page 10.

In today's world, many children entering school are already able to recite the alphabet or to recognize their own names. However, a surprising number of Kindergarteners arrive at school without many experiences in writing. They know that writing and pictures send a message, but they don't yet connect letters and sounds. We consider them to be in the *emergent* stage of literacy. Emergent readers often pretend to "read" a story as they flip through the pages of a book. Similarly, emergent writers may draw or scribble something and say, "Here's my writing." At this stage, our main focus in writing instruction is getting students to use letters and sounds. We need to spend plenty of time modeling reading and writing, building oral language and vocabulary, and inviting students to participate in a range of literacy activities.

Our emergent writers will not be able to apply most of the minilessons in this book independently; however, almost every lesson may be adapted as a teacher-guided, shared, or interactive writing experience. Remember that our students can recognize and talk about elements of effective writing long before they can demonstrate those elements on their own.

When students begin to put letters together to form words, we consider them to be *early* writers. At this stage, they are also using their knowledge of letters and sounds to decode words as they read. For most students, this stage extends from mid-Kindergarten to the middle or end of Grade 1, and students' early writing may range from representing entire words with a single letter to readable inventive spelling and some "book writing." We may even see sentences with periods, although we're just as likely to see periods at the end of every line or even after every word!

At this stage, a lot of instruction is dedicated to supporting inventive spelling and building a repertoire of conventionally spelled high-frequency words, but it's also about writing several details that stick to a topic. We worry less about publishing and correctness and more about generating ideas and using interesting words. Almost all of the minilessons in this book are adaptable to early writers.

As students acquire facility with both inventive and conventional spelling, they don't need to work as hard at writing individual words and they can pay more attention to the writer's craft. They write longer pieces and experiment with vocabulary. We call this the *developing* literacy stage. Developing readers have the stamina to read longer texts and they often enjoy beginning chapter books. Usually appearing by the end of Grade 1 or early Grade 2, the developing stage is an ideal time to introduce new genres and text forms, as well as elements of organization, word choice, and sentence variety. We also want students to start following a writing process that involves planning, drafting, revising, editing, and publishing their writing. The minilessons in this book are ideal for the developing writer.

By the time students reach the *fluent* stage, they are set to be readers and writers for life. Although older fluent readers may still function below grade level, our second- and third-graders (and sometimes first-graders) are on their way to independence. Because they are "fluent," they have more automaticity in the words they read and write. Fluent writers should be encouraged to experiment with crafting more complex sentences, organizing details, and using figurative language. Your fluent writers will be able to apply and extend any of the minilessons in this book.

At every stage of development, our children know that writing is something we do to send a message to someone else. Therefore, we teach them to think about such things as: *Will your reader understand what you've written? What details will your reader find interesting? What might your reader wonder? How can you grab your reader's attention and make him or her want to read the rest of your writing?* Who would have thought that we could talk to five- and six-year-olds about audience and purpose? But that's why we use different **text forms**: to serve different purposes and to inspire our readers to respond in different ways.

If we want to show our readers how to do something or make something, we use **procedural or "How-To" writing**. If we want to teach our readers about a topic, we use **informational or "All-About" writing**. And if we want to try to convince our readers about something that is important to us, we use **persuasive or "I-Think" writing**. In Chapters 3, 4, and 5 of this book, you will find a collection of minilesson ideas for each of these text forms.

How to Use This Book

The minilesson is only one piece of the overall writing block—the teaching piece. Most of the class period is dedicated to students writing and sharing their writing. In Chapters 1 and 2 of this book, you'll find many ideas for organizing and managing the writing block, which we'll call the "Writing Workshop." There are practical tips for establishing a Writing Workshop that supports student independence and growth. You'll learn ways to transfer responsibility from teachers to students—even at the earliest stages of writing—in order to free up the teacher to offer support to individuals and small groups. There are suggestions for starting the school year in each grade and foundational minilessons to teach different aspects of the writing process, from inventive spelling to revision and editing.

Chapters 3, 4, and 5 focus on minilesson ideas for teaching the **three major nonfiction text forms: procedural, informational, and persuasive writing**. The first minilesson in each chapter introduces the unique structure and conventions of that text form. Then students are invited to write a "benchmark" piece that enables their teacher to assess what they know and can do in order to plan instruction. Other minilessons for each text form include topic generation, planning and prewriting, organizing details, and revising for writer's craft. At the end of each chapter is a four-level rubric that may be used as an assessment tool and a guide for instruction.

Readers of my previous books, *Marvelous Minilessons for Teaching Beginning Writing, K-3* and *Marvelous Minilessons for Teaching Intermediate Writing, Grades 4-6*, will recognize a few parallels between this book and those. But here are some features that make this book unique:

- Each minilesson in this book begins with a learning goal based on a specific writing strategy.
- Most of the lessons focus on the development of ideas, the organization of details, and the craft of writing, rather than spelling and conventions.
- The lessons are structured around teacher modeling and instruction (I DO), some guided practice in large or small groups (WE DO), and independent application (YOU DO).
- The guided practice components of the lessons usually take the form of shared or interactive writing. In shared writing, the students collaboratively compose the text, while the teacher scribes. In interactive writing, the group composes the text together, but the students take turns doing the writing.
- Some lessons may take more than the requisite ten-minute timeframe. Feel free to end a minilesson midway or continue it another day.
- Most lessons include examples of what I would actually say to students; you'll find this "teacher talk" in italics embedded in the minilessons.
- Specific developmental stages for each lesson have not been identified, for a number of reasons. I believe that most of the lessons are not appropriate for emergent writers (i.e., writers who are not yet able to connect letters and sounds) to apply independently. That said, I am constantly surprised by what our youngest writers can understand and achieve. So I leave it to teachers to decide which minilessons to use for their students and how to adapt each minilesson to their students' needs and developmental levels.
- Sometimes, I'll suggest a model from a professional writer, in the form of a picture book read-aloud. However, we should never use writing time for the first reading of a text. Read any book first as readers, and then revisit it as writers to analyze and apply the techniques the writer has used.
- Each of the chapters focusing on text forms concludes with a four-level rubric that may be used for assessment or evaluation.

This book is intended to offer a smorgasbord of minilesson ideas that may be used as part of a balanced diet of writing instruction. Not every minilesson will be appropriate for every class, or even every student within a class. You are encouraged to pick and choose the lessons that address your goals for individuals and small groups. These lessons are not intended to be complete units of study, but rather a bank of ideas to add to your own teaching repertoire.

Most importantly, I encourage you to *adapt* rather than *adopt* these minilessons. Make them your own and use models that work for you. Gather student samples and literature links that you'll be able to use to reinforce the writing strategies you are teaching.

In any classroom anywhere, the students will be at many different places in their writing development. Only by careful observation and assessment of our students' writing can we provide the "just in time" instruction that will scaffold our students from their current level to increasingly higher levels of sophistication and understanding.

	Writers at this stage…	Readers at this stage…
Emergent	…know that "writing" can tell a story or communicate ideas …may use pictures, scribbles, or lines to convey a message …may copy letters or even words, but do not connect symbols and sounds …often place pictures and symbols randomly on the page …rely on pictures to "tell the story" …may write their own names in conventional print	…know that print tells a story or communicates ideas …may or may not distinguish "writing" from "pictures" …do not connect letters and sounds; are unable to decode words …may "role-play" reading …read from memory, patterns, and pictures …rely on picture clues …may be able to recognize their own names in print
Early	…use letters, words, and pictures to gather and convey ideas …use inventive spelling to write most words in speaking vocabulary …spell some high-frequency words conventionally …distinguish pictures from print; begin to apply directionality and spacing …begin to use sentences and punctuation …write about topics of personal interest and experience	…use letters, words, and pictures to get information from books …decode unfamiliar words by "sounding out" …read some high-frequency words automatically …distinguish pictures from print; begin to understand directionality and spacing …begin to understand sentences as groups of words with punctuation …prefer to read about topics relating to personal experience
Developing	…may use topics beyond their own personal experience …write longer pieces with many details …write in different text forms for different purposes and for different audiences …often write details in random order, although they have a concept of beginning, middle, and end …may show a stilted writer's voice as they focus on conventions …tend to write many short, choppy (or long, run-on) sentences …demonstrate increasing mastery of spelling and conventions, with most grade-appropriate high-frequency words spelled correctly …use readable phonetic spelling	…read about imaginative and fictional as well as nonfiction topics …can cope with longer texts; begin to read chapter books …identify and appreciate different text forms …can monitor their own comprehension and begin to use strategies flexibly …start to focus more on text-level comprehension compared to word-level comprehension …begin to summarize …attend to interesting vocabulary …read many words automatically …begin to use punctuation and to read in phrases
Fluent	…write texts of increasing length and complexity …can use a variety of text forms for different purposes and audiences …plan and organize ideas for logical structure, with leads and conclusions … include rich details, elaboration, and description in their writing …consider word choice; begin to use "book language" …begin to show variety in sentence length and structure …spell many words conventionally; phonetic spelling is logical and readable …generally use capitals and basic punctuation correctly	…read texts of increasing length and complexity …can identify and navigate different types of text structures …can consider author's purpose, message, and point of view when reading …begin to interpret figurative language and literary techniques …read with increasing fluency; can access more complex sentence structures …read many words automatically; use a range of cueing systems to solve unfamiliar words …use punctuation, paragraphing, and other text supports to aid comprehension

Chapter 1   Teaching Time, Writing Time, Sharing Time

A Sample Writing Block
Allow at least 40 minutes for a writing class.
- Teaching time: 10 minutes
- Writing Time: 20+ minutes
- Sharing time: 10 minutes

Here's a simple structure for the writing block: some teaching time, some writing time, and some sharing time. A 40-minute period, for example, would comprise a 10-minute minilesson, followed by 20 minutes of student writing time, and ending with 10 minutes of sharing and celebration. Forty minutes is about the minimum amount of time we should allocate for the writing block. It will take Kindergarteners several weeks to build stamina for 20 minutes of writing, but your upper primary students will be able to handle even more writing time.

But what about the students who say they're "done" after five or ten minutes? Here's a prescription for "what-to-do-when-I'm-done" syndrome: the Writing Workshop. The golden rule of the Writing Workshop is "You're never done!" One of the first things students learn is how to manage their Writing Time— and that means being able to move from one project to another without teacher intervention.

Teaching students to plan and use their time effectively is only one of the ways that Writing Workshop supports independence and self-regulation. The workshop structure embodies learning by doing, with every participant buying in at his or her own level, and practicing and experimenting to grow and learn. The more independent our students are, the less time we teachers need to spend monitoring and managing behavior. And we can spend more time providing the instruction and support that help our students become better writers. That doesn't mean Writing Workshop is a classroom free-for-all; it does mean, however, that we need to teach, practice, reinforce, and set expectations for consistent routines. Lucy Calkins, a pioneer of the Writing Workshop, has said that Writing Workshop is a predictable structure where the unpredictable can happen (Calkins, 1983).

The Writing Workshop philosophy is based on three key principles: time, ownership, and response. Writers need regular and consistent time for writing. They need to "own" the process, from choosing their own topics to deciding which pieces to revise, edit, and publish, including the option of abandoning a piece of writing that doesn't work for them. And they need frequent feedback from peers and teachers in order to improve their craft.

However, there is no single "right" way to approach the Writing Workshop, and different teachers will devise different routines and systems that work for them and their students. Many teachers (myself included) prefer to conduct Writing Workshop with the whole class, offering additional small-group support and individual conferences as needed. Others prefer to schedule Writing Workshop in small groups, especially for beginners who might need extra one-on-one support or groups who vary significantly in their needs. But regardless of the model used, Writing Workshop sessions pretty much all boil down to the same three components: teaching time, writing time, and sharing time.

Teaching Time

The Writing Workshop usually starts with an "I DO"—a bit of explicit instruction on a writing strategy, a workshop routine, or an element of the writer's craft. This instruction usually takes the form of teacher modeling and thinking aloud, but it might also include a literature link or a student writing sample.

The challenge for teachers is to keep this teaching *brief* and *focused*. That's why we call it a *minilesson*. The lesson should be long enough to address a learning goal, but short enough to hold the students' attention. Don't feel guilty about using this time for direct instruction; not every lesson needs to be interactive. As Lucy Calkins suggests, don't waste time asking questions for which you already know the answers!

Sometimes it might even be necessary to set a timer for ten minutes, just to get used to the limited timeframe. When the timer sounds, the lesson stops; you can always continue it another day. At the beginning of the school year, most minilessons focus on classroom routines and procedures. But as the year progresses, we spend more and more time teaching the content, craft, and conventions of writing.

Research has shown that instruction in grammar (sentence structure, punctuation, parts of speech, and word usage) is *only* effective if taught in the context of reading and writing (Graham & Perrin, 2007). So scrap the morning seatwork on compound words or apostrophes and teach those important concepts as minilessons in the context of reading and writing.

The next part of the minilesson is a "WE DO" to practice the focus strategy in a supported, guided setting. This collaborative writing experience might take the form of shared writing, in which the students compose the text together while the teacher scribes, or interactive writing, in which the students take turns doing the writing as well as generating the ideas. If a collaborative writing activity prolongs the minilesson too much, then feel free to continue it another day. Be sensitive to the needs and interests of your students. Teaching time should never take away from student writing time.

Finally, establish the expectation that students will apply the focus concept in their writing that day—the "YOU DO." For example, we might say something like: *In today's Writing Workshop, you need to use at least two vivid verbs in your writing. Please take a colored pen and highlight those words.* What six- or seven- or eight-year-old doesn't love to highlight? And this little trick also enables the teacher to circulate around the classroom and take a quick look at the students' writing, assess their understanding of the concept or skill, and plan further instruction.

Writing Time

Writing time is the longest and most important part of the Writing Workshop—at least 20 minutes or more. Here's where opportunity and accountability combine to apply the writing strategies, skills, or procedures taught in the minilessons. As mentioned earlier, 20 minutes seems to be the minimum amount of time for most students to really dig into their writing—and you'll no doubt want to increase that time as the year goes on, especially for upper primary students.

During writing time, some students might be starting a piece of writing, completing a graphic organizer, or doing some reading in preparation for writing. Others might be revisiting a piece to add details or change words. Still others might be reading their writing to a partner to get some feedback or advice. Because writers need varying amounts of time at each stage of the writing process for each piece of writing, you are likely to find that your students are all at different points in the writing process at any given time. It is neither a natural process nor effective teaching to have everyone planning, drafting, revising, and editing writing on the same schedule. One of the ways we build student independence is by empowering them to decide when to begin, continue, or end a piece of writing. And the benefit for teachers is that students don't all need the same level of support at the same time.

You're Never Done Writing Workshop

> You're never "done" Writing Workshop!
> You can:
> – finish a piece
> – revise a piece
> – start a new piece

In Writing Workshop, students are responsible for using their writing time responsibly. That means that when they finish one task, they move on to another—independently and without teacher intervention. One of the first and most important routines we establish in Writing Workshop is "what to do when you're done." There are basically three choices in Writing Workshop: finish a piece you started on a previous day; make some changes or revisions to a completed draft or work in progress; or start a whole new piece of writing. Of course, other activities such as teacher or peer conferences will also take up part of the Writing Time, but three activities—start a piece, finish a piece, revise a piece—are the foundation of the Writing Workshop. Even in Kindergarten and beginning Grade 1, students are expected to use their time independently, but the routines are a little different. We teach our youngest writers that they can: add more details to their picture; add more writing; or start a new piece. No one should ever have to ask, "What do I do when I'm done?" because "When you're done, you've just begun!" All of these routines take a lot of modeling and a lot of practice, but it's well worth the time, both to build student independence and to free the teacher up to provide individual and small group support.

> **Tip for Boosting Concentration**
> Some research suggests that playing Baroque music, such as Vivaldi or Pachelbel, promotes concentration. When your body senses the even, one-beat-per-second rhythm of the music, your heart rate and pulse relax to the beat. In this calm but alert state, your mind is able to concentrate more easily.

For most of us, writing is a social activity. We share our plans or segments of our writing, ask questions, seek advice, or simply talk as we work. This opportunity for social interaction is an important part of Writing Workshop and we need to teach students how to respond to one another's writing. But some writers find concentration difficult in the midst of a buzz of conversation and movement. That's why we start writing time with ten minutes of silence, dubbed "The Quiet Ten" by author Jennifer Jacobson (2010). I like to play soft music during this time; when the music stops, the students can move about and talk with others, but the Quiet Ten involves silent, individual writing time. For students who still need a little more solitude, cardboard carrels can be used as "private offices" to separate them from the classroom milieu.

As Writing Time draws to an end, it's useful to have some sort of closing routine. Students are invited to gather to listen and respond to one another's writing during Sharing Time.

Sharing Time

One of the features of the Writing Workshop is the opportunity to share and receive feedback on one's writing from teacher and peers. Peer conferences and teacher conferences occur both formally and informally. (On pages 18–20, you will find information about Bumblebee, TAG, and Polish to Publish conferences.) Additionally, a wonderful way to conclude the Writing Workshop each day is with a special sharing and celebration time, often called "Author's Chair."

Many teachers actually have a special chair in which students sit to share their work. (In fact, some teachers call it a "share chair" because it's not limited just to Writing Workshop.) An Internet search will turn up many pictures of Author's Chairs, from simple to elaborate. I rarely use a chair, however. When possible, I like to have students stand in front of a music stand and use a microphone. The music stand functions as a podium, holding the writer's book, paper, tablet, or hand-held device. The microphone amplifies tiny voices and makes sharing time that much more special and grown-up.

Because we have just five to ten minutes for Sharing Time, only two or three students can share their writing each day. It is both a privilege and a responsibility to share one's writing and every student will take a turn. Running down the class list, I announce at the beginning of Writing Workshop the names of the two students who will share at the end of the workshop. During Writing Time, these designated students must select a piece of writing and practice reading it aloud. They may read any piece—published or draft—as long as they haven't read it to the class before in the same form. (A piece may be reread if it has been revised in some way.)

We treat these student writers just as we would any other writer. We start by telling them what we like about their writing or what they've done well. Then we ask questions about aspects of the writing that we don't understand or wish we knew more about. We call these comments "Stars" and "Wishes." At first, students commonly struggle to find the language they need in order to offer constructive feedback to another writer. It's common to hear students say, "I liked it" or "It was funny." We need to prompt students to explain these comments further to help students identify *what* they liked, *what* was funny, or *what* the writer did well. We need to give them the words they need to talk to one another about the content and craft of writing. By teaching students about the writer's craft and modeling effective feedback, we can help students build the vocabulary they need for talking about writing—their own and that of others.

Sharing Time is a gentle way to bring closure to the Writing Workshop—and a powerful routine for helping students acquire the language and attitudes of writers.

Supporting Independence

Empowering youngsters to make choices about their learning not only increases motivation for that particular task—it also reduces behavior issues and supports quality, completion, and creative endeavor for that task, and even promotes the general well-being of the learner (Kohn, 1993).

There are several ways in which Writing Workshop supports independent learning. We've already discussed the "Golden Rule" of Writing Workshop: "You're never done!" Whether students are expected to "finish a piece, revise a piece, start a piece" or "add more details to your picture, add more writing, start a new piece," we are building self-regulation. Two other ways to support independence are: self-selection of topics and keeping a writing log to plan effective use of time.

Choosing Topics for Writing

With the exception of occasional guided writing tasks that are assigned to practice a strategy, even our youngest students are expected to choose what they're going to write about and what form it will take. At first, this is challenging for some students, especially those who haven't had a rich range of life experiences— or those who aren't accustomed to making independent choices.

Writers are more engaged when they write about topics that matter to them. They write more and they write better. Research has shown that children who are interested in a topic pay more attention, sustain that attention for longer periods of time, and acquire more knowledge than they do with topics of less interest (Hidi & Anderson, 2014).

I often hear teachers say: "But my students don't have anything to write about!" Students need to see that anything can be an interesting topic, depending on how the writer treats that topic. (Poet Shel Silverstein has written poems about everything from hiccups to boxes—and even a toilet plunger!) It's important that we model writing about everyday topics and show students how to use rich details to make topics interesting to readers. Consider using shared school experiences such as a recent school assembly, an interesting class read-aloud, a playground dispute, or a topic of study.

The truth is, the more a person writes, the easier it is to think of something to write about. People who write for a living will tell you that they have more ideas in their heads than they'll ever have an opportunity to use. On the other hand, the last thing we want is for students to waste valuable Writing Time trying to choose a topic. In this book, you'll find minilesson ideas for choosing topics for each of the three focus text forms.

A very simple tool to aid topic selection is the **Big Ideas Bag** like the one shown on the left. Post a sheet of chart paper in a visible place in the classroom and add a few topics each day, based on learning experiences in the classroom. Anything ranging from a science lesson to a family outing can be potential topics for writing. When the sheet is full, simply cut it into strips and put the strips into a large gift bag from the dollar store, as shown in the photograph. Anyone stuck for an idea has the option of drawing a topic from the Big Ideas Bag. There's only one rule: if you choose to draw a topic from the Big Ideas Bag, you must write about it. We know that every topic in that bag is a shared classroom experience that everyone will have the necessary background experience to write about.

Authentic Writing Tasks vs. Writing "Prompts"

Some teachers believe that students need to be given writing prompts. It is true that we occasionally need to have our students write something specific, such as a thank-you letter to the guide who gave the class a tour of the museum or a short guided writing assignment to practice a focus strategy. The difference between these tasks and a traditional "prompt" (e.g., "Tell about a time when...") is authentic *audience* and *purpose*. Our children have plenty of opportunities to learn to write to prompts in content area subjects (where they are "writing to learn" as opposed to "learning to write"). When we tell students to write a math journal entry explaining how to add two-digit numbers or assign a lab report on a science experiment, we're teaching students to write to a prompt. But truly powerful writing comes from topics that the writer actually cares about and knows about.

Keeping a Writing Log

Following the workshop minilesson, students should plan how they are going to use their Writing Time. In Kindergarten and Grade 1, that plan is likely to involve simply telling someone else what they're going to write about; in upper primary, students are taught to complete a writing log. (A template may be found on page 21).

For the first few minutes of Writing Time, students in Grades 2 and 3 (and sometimes upper Grade 1) will record the date and what they plan to work on. Often the plan will start with some sort of guided writing task from the minilesson, such as "Add an *all-in-all ending* to my All-About Snails piece." Because this task is unlikely to occupy the entire Writing Time, the writer should also plan what he/she is going to do next, such as "Start to collect facts for All-About Lego" or "Edit How-To Score a Goal in Soccer and put it in the editing basket." This planning routine is an important part of Writing Time, as it helps writers focus their attention and make effective use of their time. As soon as they record their plans, students should leave their writing logs out for the teacher to see and then get started on their writing.

As students complete their writing logs, teachers should circulate among them to check their writing plans. If students' plans look satisfactory, don't interrupt them! Just let each student keep on writing and move on to the next student. Use this time to check on plans that seem inadequate or unclear and to help students who can't seem to get started.

When students are comfortable with recording their plans each day, you can add a reflection component to the writing log. Allow a couple of minutes at the end of Writing Time for students to record what they actually accomplished. (On the other hand, you may decide not to have them complete a written reflection; instead, as students gather for Sharing Time, give them a minute or two to tell a partner what they did in Writing Time.)

Of course, explicitly teaching students how to complete their writing logs is an essential minilesson in the early days of the Writing Workshop and it may take several days of modeling and guided practice before students are able to plan their time effectively. Start by displaying a blank writing log and think aloud as you record your hypothetical writing plans for the day. Then have students talk to a partner before completing their own writing logs.

The writing log is not only a useful planning tool for students, it is a valuable assessment tool for teachers, especially when you can compare students' plans and reflections. The writing log can offer a snapshot of how well students use their Writing Time and what stages of the writing process they are accomplishing.

Managing Materials

One of the many great things about Writing Workshop is that you don't need any special materials. I tend to prefer individual sheets of paper that may or may not be combined into a booklet. In Kindergarten, we use blank, unlined paper; at this stage, writers often integrate drawing and "writing" and are experimenting with directionality and spacing.

By Grade 1, many children are ready for lined paper. (That's not to say they can't continue to use unlined paper, if they prefer.) Indicators that a child might be ready for lines include: evidence of directionality in writing; drawing after writing rather than before, or not drawing at all; or, filling the page with several details.

From Kindergarten on, we have the students write with skinny markers or even pens. That's how grown-up and special Writing Workshop is! Not to mention the fact that we want to eliminate *erasing*, which too often occupies far too much of some students' time and energy. That doesn't mean they can't change their minds or their writing. Teaching students to use **The Strikethrough** (page 35) to delete material they want to change is cleaner, more efficient, and more positive than erasing something they've written.

By upper primary grades, we want students to take responsibility for managing their own paper. That's where the **Writing Folder** comes in. There are many workable systems for writing portfolios. What works for me is a three-pocket folder labeled: **Writing Ideas** (to store planning or topic sheets or a writer's notebook); **Works in Progress** (drafts that are incomplete); and **Finished Drafts**.

To make a writing folder, simply find a large sheet of tagboard or Bristol board. Fold up the bottom third to form a pocket. Fold the entire folder into three vertical folds. Use a long-armed stapler to separate the three pockets. Label the pockets and have students decorate their own covers and laminate them, if possible. Now your folders are ready to go—and they store easily in storage cubes readily available from your nearest big box store.

Even a writing folder can get unwieldy if it contains too many pieces of paper. That's why students store only three writing pieces at a time. My rule of thumb is: ***Draft three, publish one.*** For every three pieces they write, students select only one piece to revise, edit, and take to publication. The flip side of this rule is that students must write three unique drafts for every published piece. Note that the students themselves choose which pieces they're going to publish. These are the pieces on which we'll have formal (TAG) conferences (see page 18) and on which students will do both revision and editing.

It should be noted that we're talking about developing and fluent writers here (mostly Grades 2 and 3, but possibly Grade 1). I rarely have emergent and early writers in Kindergarten or Grade 1 polish and publish their writing; their work is generally just one draft, although they are always encouraged to add details to words or pictures or even use a strikethrough to change words and details. The writing process at different stages of development and the publication journey are discussed in greater detail in the next chapter.

The Teacher's Role

With all this student independence, what's left for the teacher to do? Writing Workshop is a wonderful opportunity to offer just-in-time teaching in the form of individual writing conferences. During the students' Writing Time, I'm busy conducting Bumblebee, TAG, and Polish to Publish conferences.

Bumblebee Conferences

I've called these conferences many different names over the years, but the principle remains essentially the same: I "buzz" around the room like a bumblebee, alighting at every desk or table to offer the writer a quick consultation.

For early primary writers (in Kindergarten or Grade 1), I spend most of Writing Time "buzzing" around, inviting students to *Tell me what your writing says* or *Tell me what's happening in your picture*. After the student "reads" his or her piece to me, I try to give a piece of advice to move the writing forward; for beginning writers, this advice usually involves adding a detail to a picture or a piece of writing, such as: *What's your dog's name? Can you add that detail to your writing? Can you think of what's missing from your picture of taking your dog for a walk? Why don't you add a leash to your picture?* Sometimes my comments involve the conventions of writing: *Dad starts with D, just like David on our name wall. Please add a D for Dad right here in your curly writing.*

Once we've established a high-frequency Word Wall, the words on the wall become "no-excuse words" and students are always expected to write them using conventional spelling. Thus, I'll often use the Bumblebee conference to point out errors in the spelling of Word Wall words, such as: *You have two Word Wall words here. Please find them and write them in book writing.*

Upper-level primary writers don't need quite as much ongoing support during writing. As well, we need to allow these students more time for revision and editing conferences, so the Bumblebee conference has a somewhat different function. As Writing Time begins, I buzz around the room to take a look at each student's writing log and to make sure everyone is getting started. If I have a question for the student about his or her plans for the day, I'll stop and pose it, but I try to avoid interrupting a student who is already writing. At this point, I focus on students who have a problem to deal with or who seem unable to get started. Once everyone is off to a good start, I can dedicate my time to revision and editing conferences.

TAG (Revision) Conferences

The TAG conference may very well be my favorite part of the Writing Workshop, because it gives me one-on-one time with writers to target specific needs in their writing.

The TAG conference is actually a *revision* conference in preparation for publishing, so the focus is on content, clarity, and craft; there will be an opportunity to look at spelling and conventions later. I always start by identifying strengths in the writing, *telling* the writer things he or she has done well. Then I will *ask* the writer some questions about the writing, either to clarify the content or to discuss decisions the writer has made. For example, I might say, *What happened when your cat jumped in the bathtub?* or *Why did you decide to end the piece in this way?*

Writing Conference Tip
Here's a tip when conferring with writers from Kindergarten to College: Never leave a conference without asking the writer to state what change(s) he or she plans to make to the writing.

The acronym **TAG** stands for:
- **T**ell something you like.
- **A**sk questions.
- **G**ive advice.

Finally I will *give some advice*—one or two suggestions to help make the writing more interesting, more coherent, or more eloquent.

For most student writing, I could offer plenty of suggestions; however, I'm going to limit myself to just a couple of things the writer will be able to apply to future writing. I don't want to put words in the writer's mouth; rather, I am going to make general suggestions that he or she can apply to the writing, such as: *Why don't you add the detail about how your cat got out of the yard?* or *We've talked about different ways to end a piece of writing. Please replace "The End" with an ending that ties the bow on the present for a reader.*

Sample TAG Conference to Help Prepare a Writing Piece for Publication

Generally, we only have time for TAG conferences on pieces of writing that are going to be published. When a student has decided to take a piece to publication, he or she places it in my TAG conference basket. The student moves on to other writing until I call him or her up for the conference. This gives me time to review the piece and prepare my comments before the meeting.

If I'm going to give useful comments, I need to prepare ahead of time; I only have three or four minutes to spend with that student, so I need to make those minutes count. After the TAG conference, the student is expected to make the revisions we discussed. Although my recommendations are labeled "advice," they are not optional! The whole point of the exercise is to build strategies that will not only make each student's writing stronger, but that can be applied to other writing down the road.

However brief, the TAG conference provides an opportunity to spend precious time with students and to offer the just-in-time teaching that will nudge each student to higher levels of sophistication.

> My Grandma's Cat
> My grandma has a cat. It had a baby. My grandma's cat scratched me. The baby is black and scared a lot. The cats knocked down the Christmas tree. There was glass all over the place. The big cat is kind of mean.
> – Miranda S

T: *You gave lots of interesting details that stick to your topic. Your detail about the cats knocking down the Christmas tree was especially interesting.*
A: *I'm wondering what happened when the cats knocked down the Christmas tree. How did that happen?*
G: *Remember that elaboration is adding details to other details. Would you please elaborate on how the cats knocked down the Christmas tree? What might be a better title for this piece now?*

Polish to Publish (Editing) Conferences

The final step before taking a piece of writing to publication is repairing conventions. It's much easier for a reader to navigate a piece of writing when the writer has used conventional spelling and grammar. However, our primary students' writing is likely to always contain some inventive spelling, even in published writing. That's often part of their charm! Our challenge as teachers is to decide what a particular writer needs to fix, what elements are teachable, and what may be left alone.

After a writer has completed the required revisions based on the TAG conference, that student is responsible for the final conference, known as "Polish to Publish." This means **Editing Your Own Writing** (page 38) by reading each sentence twice to listen and look for errors in spelling and grammar. Don't expect miracles! It's very difficult for young (and old) writers to spot errors in their own work, but it's an important process to teach students. When the writer has completed his or her own edits, he or she once again submits the writing, this time placing it into the Polish to Publish basket, for a final teacher conference.

The teacher's task in this conference is to review the piece of writing to determine what that particular writer needs to fix. Choosing which errors to fix can be arbitrary and will differ for different writers and different situations. There are no hard and fast rules, except that any high-frequency words that are on the Word Wall or that have otherwise been taught **must** be fixed. Once they have been taught, these are "no-excuse words" and they must always be spelled conventionally.

Otherwise, we look for spelling errors and grammatical structures that the writer should already know or that are teachable in a short conference. Are there any patterns in the student's errors? Is there a guideline (such as *i before e*) that you might review? Be selective. Sitting with a student to correct error after error is not a good use of either your time or your student's. Reviewing a small number of errors enables a better chance of a student's retention and application in future writing.

The Writing Workshop is an important routine for students and teachers because it meets every student where he or she is. Often our most vulnerable learners respond best to the Writing Workshop because, for once, the work isn't too hard. Every student can participate, or "buy in," at his or her own level and progress at an individual pace to ever higher levels of achievement.

To Fix or Not to Fix?

Should the teacher act as the final copyeditor on all students' published writing—in other words, make all final corrections? I make that call based on how "public" the published piece will be. If it's going to be published for classroom use only, then I allow errors in conventions. If the writing is going out into the world, where readers may not understand the process taught to young writers, I tend to fix many, if not all, errors. In this way, readers can focus on the message of the writing, not the number of spelling mistakes.

Writing Log Template

Date	What I Plan to Work on Today	What I Got Done Today

Chapter 2   Let's Get Started! Day 1 and Beyond

It's the first week of school and already time to launch our Writing Workshop. So, where do we start?

We have two priorities during the first weeks of Writing Workshop: to encourage our students to get their ideas down on paper—even if it's drawing and scribble writing (sometimes called "driting"); and to establish the classroom routines and procedures that will build independence and self-regulation for the rest of the year. As we discussed in Chapter 1, one of the great things about Writing Workshop is that everyone can participate at his or her own level. Not to mention the fact that we don't need a lot of elaborate materials—just something to write on and something to write with. These are all great reasons why Writing Workshop should be one of those first-week-of-school routines!

For every grade level, I like to start the year with personal narrative writing—stories about students' own lives and experiences. This is the easiest kind of writing because the topics and details are right there in the students' background knowledge. And while the students are writing, I can focus on introducing or reinforcing the routines of Writing Workshop.

Although the foundations of Writing Workshop are the same from Kindergarten to college (i.e., Teaching Time, Writing Time, Sharing Time), the launch of the Writing Workshop looks a little different in Kindergarten compared to the upper grades. In this chapter, you'll find some suggested routines for the first few weeks of school along with some foundational minilessons to get your students writing. The minilesson titles are in bold print throughout the chapter, with the lessons themselves following at the end of the chapter.

Writing in Kindergarten

When our children show up at the door of Kindergarten, we usually have no idea what they know and understand about letters and sounds. Writing is a great way to find out.

I want to teach this fundamental concept to Kindergarteners: we write to send a message, tell a story, or give information to someone else. Every one of them is a writer and the rest of us are their readers. I tell students that Writing Workshop is

Page	Minilesson Name	Learning Goal Students will be able to…
30	Topic and Details	…choose topics and add appropriate details.
31	Bubble Gum or Book Writing	…use inventive spelling for words they don't know how to spell conventionally.
32	Sticky Dot Details	…generate more than one detail about a topic.
33	Adding on Details	…revise writing by adding details at the end.
34	Pushing in Details	…revise writing by inserting details with a caret.
35	The Strikethrough	…revise by drawing a line through text and changing the words.
36	Stretching the Paper	…revise writing by tucking in chunks of information.
37	Pruning Your Writing	…revise writing by deleting unnecessary details.
38	Editing Your Own Writing	…edit their own writing for conventions.

an important routine that we will do every day in school. First, it will be my turn to write and then it will be their turn. In fact, it will be their job to write every day during Writing Workshop.

Most of our Kindergarteners arrive at school as *emergent* writers, who pretend to write by scribbling and/or drawing. By mid-year, most have become *early* writers, who can write by connecting letters and sounds and who are ready for the minilessons in this book.

Right from the first days of school, I model three ways to write in Kindergarten: "curly [scribble] writing," "ABC writing," and "book writing." Just as in the books we read, we will tell stories with pictures and writing. I describe my "topic" and my "details." Then I draw a picture and demonstrate "writing" with scribbles, a few alphabet letters, and conventional spelling. Together, we all try each type of writing and I tell students that they can use whatever kind of writing works best for them. (This lesson is described more fully in my books *Marvelous Minilessons for Teaching Beginning Writing, K-3* and *Read, Write, Play, Learn: Literacy Instruction in Today's Kindergarten.*)

I like to teach the alphabet using the children's names—one letter a day—and we practice printing the letters as we use them to form words. As we add letters to our repertoire, I encourage students to use these letters in their writing. And as I buzz around the room in **Bumblebee conferences** (as described on page 18), I'm constantly nudging students to add more letters to their writing: *Dog starts just like David on our name wall…. Can you hear the ending sound of d-o-g? What letter would you use to represent that sound?* Once students have a

---

Transcribing with Purpose

How important is providing a "transcription" of a child's writing? Sometimes we record the child's "reading" of his or her own writing for evaluation or portfolio purposes. Sometimes we want to hold on to a memorable comment to share with parents. But when we transcribe, we do it for ourselves, not for the students. The students really learn nothing from having the "book writing" beside their own. So, before transcribing, stop and think about why you're doing it. If you've got a good purpose, then go ahead. Otherwise, save your time for tasks that actually make your students better readers, writers, and thinkers.

repertoire of alphabet letters under their belts and are beginning to connect the letters to sounds in logical ways, we consider them to be *early* writers. Now it's time to focus on inventive spelling, as shown in **Bubble Gum or Book Writing** (page 31) and leave scribble writing behind.

Writing is all about choosing a **Topic and Details** (page 30). In Kindergarten, we always tell what we're going to write about before we put our ideas on paper. When children share their ideas in a group, it helps them organize their thinking (and it often inspires those students who can't think of what to write about). Later, I'll teach them about **Adding on Details** (page 33) to a picture or to their writing. This is the foundation for Writing Workshop routines (See "You're Never Done Writing Workshop," page 13). I teach the students that when they feel they're finished working on a piece of writing, it's their responsibility to plan what they're going to do next. They can go back to any previous piece and add some details to a picture or add some more "writing." Alternatively, they have the option of starting a new piece of writing.

For Kindergarten and Grade 1 writers, every piece of writing is a work in progress; we rarely "publish" writing, but we often revisit writing to add details. The writing process in Kindergarten generally consists of drawing a picture, adding some writing, and then putting their name and date on the page.

Writing in Grade 1

The majority of our first graders arrive at our door as *early* writers; they know and can use a range of alphabet letters, especially consonants. Therefore, I don't really encourage scribble writing or random letters, except in unique circumstances. I want to establish the expectation, right from day one, that students can write any word they can say. I will help them with words, if they ask for help, but only if they try the words themselves first. I can then work with the students individually to help them use a range of spelling strategies to write the word conventionally.

I hope that my first graders have already had plenty of experience with inventive spelling in Kindergarten, but it's still very important to teach, review, and reinforce **Bubble Gum or Book Writing** (page 31) right from the start of the year. I call inventive spelling "bubble gum writing" because it involves stretching out a word like a piece of bubble gum and writing a letter for every sound that is heard. For most students, this lesson is a review from Kindergarten, but in Grade 1 we nudge students to include more medial vowels, apply letter patterns, and build a repertoire of high-frequency words. (Once a word has been studied and placed on the high-frequency Word Wall, it's a "no-excuse word" and students are expected to spell it conventionally—every time.)

It's been shown that children who are encouraged to spell inventively not only use a greater variety of words, but actually become better spellers down the road (Clarke, 1988). That's because they learn to experiment with letters and sounds and to problem-solve about how our language goes together. Experimenting with logical inventive spelling that represents every sound with a letter or letter combination is an important milestone on the road to literacy.

Most of our first graders already know how to write by adding captions to pictures. Now we want them to generate more than one detail about a topic. Good writing is all about **Topic and Details** (page 30) and the *best* writing is full of interesting or "surprising" details. **Sticky Dot Details** (page 32) teaches students

---

A Helpful Spelling Routine

What about those students who won't write anything unless they can get help with spelling? I will help them with the spelling of a word, but only if they try to spell it on their own first. That's a non-negotiable routine. Then we can work with the child's inventive spelling of the word to celebrate what he or she has done correctly and apply some strategies (e.g., look for a part you know, flip the vowel, etc.) in order to spell the entire word conventionally.

---

to place a dot after each detail they write; it's a simple tool that motivates students to bulk up their writing, while sticking to their chosen topics. Most first graders aren't yet ready for graphic organizers or other planning tools. However, we can teach them to plan by "pre-telling," or telling a partner what they're going to write.

The first weeks of school in Grade 1 are dedicated to establishing Writing Workshop routines (see "You're Never Done Writing Workshop," page 13). We want to give students a repertoire of strategies for revisiting a piece of writing and **Adding on Details** (page 33). Grade 1 writers can also learn to insert additional information into their text by using a caret and **Pushing in Details** (page 34) or to change details by using **The Strikethrough** (page 35).

At some point in Grade 1, we will introduce **Editing Your Own Writing** (page 38) but for the most part, correcting the spelling of known high-frequency words and distinguishing capital and lower-case letters are the main expectations for conventions. We will also work on sentence structures as the year goes on.

There is no learning to be gained in having first graders recopy their writing for publication. There's more value in having them do more first-draft writing. Thus, the writing process for much of Grade 1 looks like this: tell what you're going to write; write and draw (or draw and write); add details to the ending of a piece; and repair Word Wall words.

Writing in Grades 2, 3, and Beyond

The first thing we want to know in Grades 2 and 3 is what our students know and can do as writers. One of my favorite first-day minilessons is **Love It or Loathe It** (page 83). Students complete a simple graphic organizer that provides them with a repertoire of topics for writing, based on subjects they feel strongly about, either positively or negatively. For the rest of the week, the students write about topics chosen from these lists. Each day, writers have the option of starting a new topic, finishing a piece from another day, or fixing up a piece written previously. Thus, we start building the foundation of Writing Workshop.

As the students write independently each day, I teach minilessons on the routines and procedures of Writing Workshop. By the end of the week, I have a collection of writing samples from each student to use for a benchmark assessment. A rubric like the one on page 29 helps me ascertain which strategies my students have mastered and which strategies I need to focus on as I plan instruction.

Your students will likely have had some experience with Writing Workshop before they enter your second- or third-grade classroom. If not, it might be necessary to go back to basics. Tell the students that each Writing Workshop will begin with everyone gathering together for a short lesson on a strategy that writers use. Then they will have time to do their own writing to try out that strategy. (Just like in Kindergarten: *First I'm going to do some writing, then you're going to do some writing.*) We spend a lot of time simply modeling and practicing the routines described in the section "You're Never Done Writing Workshop" (page 13), which include finishing an incomplete piece, making changes to an existing draft, or starting a new piece. It's really important that this independence is firmly established as early as possible.

Distributing and decorating writing folders is a great motivator for writing. A three-pocket **Writing Folder** was described on page 17. It has pockets to store Writing Ideas, Works in Progress, and Completed Drafts. And let's not forget that most grown-up of Writing Workshop tools: THE PEN. Allowing primary students to use a pen for writing conveys a sense of the importance and sophistication of Writing Workshop; but the main benefit is, of course, to avoid *erasing!* Instead, we teach students to use **The Strikethrough** (page 35), which involves drawing a single line through the unwanted word or section of text and just continuing with the writing.

At the beginning of the year, our focus is on first-draft writing as we establish the routines and procedures of the Writing Workshop. Gradually, however, we begin to incorporate the whole writing process: planning, drafting, revising, editing, and publishing. It's important to differentiate between *revising* writing to make it more clear and interesting and *editing* writing to correct spelling and language conventions.

You might wish to introduce several revision strategies during the first month of school—or you might choose to introduce them gradually as needed. One thing we know is that recopying the entire piece for every revision is laborious and unnecessary; several minilessons at the end of this chapter offer techniques for revising without rewriting. Your Grades 2 and 3 students should already be familiar with the easiest of revision strategies: adding details to the end of a piece of writing. As well, you will want to review **Pushing in Details** (page 34) and use of **The Strikethrough** (page 35) to change or delete details. **Stretching the Paper** (page 36) is a technique for increasing writing space when several details or a chunk of information must be added. **Pruning Your Writing** (page 37) involves removing details—the most challenging of all revision strategies for our primary students, for whom every detail is a labor of love—or at least a labor.

The final step before sharing a piece of writing with a reader ("publishing") is editing for conventions, e.g., capitalization, word usage, punctuation, and spelling. I'm afraid I haven't found a way to make this step less painful, but **Editing Your Own Writing** (page 38) can at least make it a little more manageable.

By the end of the first month, you will have laid valuable groundwork for students' independence throughout the year. Now you can focus more on the craft of writing and the introduction of new text forms, such as those explained in Chapters 3, 4, and 5 of this book.

> It's important to differentiate between revising (making the writing more clear and interesting by adding, changing, moving, or removing details) and editing (correcting spelling, grammar, and punctuation).

> **Double-space/Single-side**
> Establish the habit of writing on only one side of the page and leaving a space between each line to allow room for revision.

Word Processing or Not?

Throughout most of this book, it is assumed that students will be doing their writing by hand. But by Grades 2 and 3, many of your students will be proficient enough with a keyboard to use word processing when they write or revise their drafts. However, students should not use word processing if their keyboarding skills (or lack thereof) interfere with their thinking and composing, especially at the drafting stage. In most primary classrooms, students tend to handwrite their initial drafts, but they sometimes have the option of word processing their published copies. Be aware, however, that word processing will not necessarily eliminate spelling errors; in fact, many students make errors when word processing that they don't make when they write (or print) by hand!

	EMERGENT (K)	EARLY (K-1)	DEVELOPING (Grades 1-3)	FLUENT (Grades 2-3)
PRE-WRITING	Tell what you're going to write.	Tell what you're going to write.	Use planning tools or graphic organizers.	
DRAFTING	Draw and write. • Scribbling • Letters • Book writing	Write and draw (in either order).	Pour out ideas on paper in writing. • Double-space/Single-side	
REVISING	Add more details to the picture or the writing.	Add details at the end.	Add, change, move, or delete details to make the writing more interesting, clear, and powerful.	
EDITING	Add some letters for sounds that are heard.	Fix known high-frequency words (i.e., Word Wall words).	Fix capitals, usage, punctuation, and spelling.	
PUBLISHING	Read the writing to others.	Read the writing to others.	Word process or rewrite a polished copy to share with an audience.	

The Publishing Journey

Publishing, in educational parlance, is simply sharing writing with an audience. Although there is limited value in having *emergent* and *early* writers correct and recopy their writing, they can and should be encouraged to share their writing with others. By the time students reach the *developing* and *fluent* stages (by the beginning of Grade 2, for most students), they should be able to revise and edit selected drafts for publication. The publishing journey has already been briefly discussed in Chapter 1, in the context of teacher TAG conferences. Here are some tips to help make the journey a smooth one:

- Not every piece of writing needs to be polished and published. I encourage students to draft three pieces for every piece that is published. In this way, they will always have writing in their folders for practicing strategies that have been taught. As well, they'll have choices about which pieces merit publication.
- Students choose the pieces they are going to publish. It's a rather difficult concept to think that it's our *best* writing that we change and rework and correct to share with an audience (unlike other subject areas, where it's the incorrect or incomplete work that needs fixing). As students complete three pieces of writing, they select the one that will be taken to publication.

The Problem with Peer Editing

I rarely have students edit each other's work for conventions. Often the peer editor doesn't know any more about the correct spelling and punctuation than the writer does! And if they are already competent spellers, it's a waste of their own writing time to be correcting someone else's work. Finally, it should be a teacher's professional decision about which errors should be corrected and which may be left as is at this stage.

(Depending on the individual students and the amount of time allocated for Writing Workshop, most students in Grades 2 and 3 will complete at least three drafts and one published piece each month.)

- When a student has chosen a piece for publication, he or she places it in the teacher's TAG conference basket and moves on to other writing while waiting for the teacher conference. The **TAG conference**, described more fully on page 18, is an opportunity for teacher and student to discuss the merits of the work and what might be done to improve it. The primary focus of this conference is content: the clarity, completeness, and effectiveness of the details. If all this seems to be in place, the teacher will discuss the writer's craft—vocabulary, fluency, and voice. This is not the time to look at spelling and conventions.

- You may choose to incorporate peer conferences into the publication journey. In Grades 2 and 3, we teach students to offer **Stars** (praise or compliments for the writing) and **Wishes** (questions for clarity or requests for more information) to one another. This provides positive reinforcement for the writer, but also identifies possible points of confusion for a reader that the writer might wish to correct.

- Fixing up the spelling and conventions is what we call "Polish to Publish." We correct conventions as a courtesy for our readers, to make our writing easier to read. After they have had a chance to make the required revisions, students should take time to attend to **Editing Your Own Writing** (page 38). After their self-edits, students place the piece of writing in the teacher's Polish to Publish basket for a final editing conference (see page 19). At this point, the teacher will decide which errors should reasonably be corrected and which may be left as is. This means that sometimes children's work will go to publication with some inventive spelling or errors in other conventions. The extent to which a writing piece must be corrected really depends on how "public" the writing will be. (See page 20 for a discussion of teachers as editors.) Remember that the priority here is not a perfect piece of writing, but a learning opportunity for children.

- My favorite way to publish writing is to have it word processed and added to an ongoing collection. (A three-ring binder, folder, or coiled booklet may be used to hold published writing.)

- When a piece of writing is published, the journey is complete. All writing is submitted to the teacher for evaluation. The published piece is added to the student's collection of published work and the rough drafts are sent home. And a new writing journey begins.

What about Evaluation?

Whether we like it or not, evaluation of student progress is a critical part of teaching and learning. The key to effective evaluation is starting with learning goals. When we identify what we want students to know and be able to do, we can determine whether students have met those goals. Evaluation measures student progress toward the goals that have been set for them.

It's important that we only evaluate students on what they have been taught. For example, there's no point in scoring a piece of writing on the effectiveness of a lead or a conclusion if we haven't given any lessons on leads or conclusions. On the other hand, if we've set an expectation that Word Wall words should always be written in "book writing," then we evaluate the extent to which previously taught words are spelled conventionally. In other words, the goals of the lessons we have taught form the criteria for evaluating our students' work.

Because evaluation of writing tends to be subjective rather than "right or wrong," we often use rubrics and checklists as a guide. It's important that rubrics evaluate what students have been taught and it's quite easy to set up a three- or four-point scale for each learning goal. A sample four-level rubric based on the "six traits" of effective writing—ideas, organization, voice, word choice, sentence fluency, and conventions—appears below.

Sample Assessment Rubric

Unlike evaluation, which involves assigning a grade or judging student work, assessment involves gathering information for the purpose of planning instruction. The following rubric is based on the six traits framework and is a useful assessment tool. If you collect writing samples during the first week of school and thereafter, you can use this rubric to help determine your students' level of proficiency and what instruction they need.

	4	3	2	1
Ideas/ Content	Focused main idea with strong supporting details and unique treatment of ideas	Clear main idea with some supporting details	Minimal support for main idea; may have irrelevant details	Limited content or details
Organization	Well-structured organization; effective lead; adequate conclusion	Coherent, orderly structure, with some effort at lead and conclusion	Some details may be out of place; inadequate lead and/or conclusion	Limited details; no lead or conclusion
Voice	The writing has personality. It speaks to the reader and may evoke emotion.	Tone is appropriate, with occasional glimmers of voice.	Generally pleasant but not distinctive voice	The writing sounds stilted/"mechanical".
Word Choice	Consistent use of sophisticated and carefully chosen words	Attempt at some descriptive words	Word choice is appropriate but mundane; mostly "conversational" language.	Word choice may be immature and repetitive.
Sentence Fluency	A variety of sentences with different lengths and structures makes the writing sound rhythmical to the ear.	Sentences are correct, but most are similar in length and style; they create a smooth sound.	Mostly simple and compound sentences and repeated structures create a choppy sound.	Writing exhibits an overall lack of sentence sense.
Conventions	Superior mastery of conventions for developmental level	General mastery of conventions appropriate to the developmental level	Control of most conventions appropriate to the developmental level	Inadequate mastery of conventions for the developmental level

Topic and Details

LEARNING GOAL: Students will be able to choose their own topics and add related details in writing.

I DO: Remind students that a *topic* is what we write about and *details* are the information about that topic. You might wish to revisit a simple picture book to distinguish the concepts of topic and details.

*Each time writers start a piece of writing, they have to choose a **topic** to write about. Here are three things to think about when choosing a topic:*

- *Is the topic interesting to me?*
- *Do I know enough about the topic to write about it?*
- *Will a reader be interested in reading about this topic?*

You might like to write about things you have done or things you can do, such as scoring a goal in hockey or visiting Grandma. But those aren't the only things you can write about. Anything can be a topic for writing, if you make it interesting to yourself and to your reader. You do that by adding interesting details.

Shel Silverstein's poems can be an example of making ordinary topics interesting by adding rich details. Consider his poem "Hat" from *Where the Sidewalk Ends*. Silverstein took a boring topic—a toilet plunger —and made it interesting to a reader by using a "surprising" detail about the boy putting it on his head, thinking it was a hat.

WE DO: Use a sheet of chart paper to introduce an ongoing Topic List to be posted in the classroom for students to reference if they need help with a topic. Together, talk about discussions or experiences they've already had in the classroom together that might be topics for writing, such as: "Interesting facts about snails"; or "What's the difference between a triangle and a circle?" or "What to do if someone 'butts' you in line." This list should be ongoing and you and your students can add to it every day. When the chart paper is full, cut the paper into topic strips and add these strips to the **Big Ideas Bag** (see page 15).

YOU DO: Tell students that they will be expected to think of their own topics for writing, just as grown-up writers do. Anything can be a topic for writing, as long as writers use interesting details. Any time students can't think of a topic, they can look at the Topic List posted in the classroom for ideas or draw a topic from the Big Ideas Bag. Give students a few minutes to talk to a partner about what topic they're going to write about today and what details they might include.

Topic and Details

A *topic* is what we write about and *details* are the information we provide about that topic. Make your details interesting!

Bubble Gum or Book Writing

Learning Goal: Students will be able to use conventional spelling when possible and inventive spelling for words they don't yet know how to spell.

I DO: *When you are writing, you use lots of different words. Sometimes you already know how to write a word in book writing. Sometimes you might be able to find the word you need on the Word Wall or someplace else in the classroom. But if you don't know how to write a word in book writing, there's something you can do on your own: just think of the word in your mouth as a piece of bubble gum that you can stretch out as you listen for all the sounds. We call that "bubble gum writing."*

Use modeled writing to demonstrate inventive spelling as part of connected text, thinking aloud about *why* and *how* it's done. *I'm going to show you how I can use bubble gum words in my writing. With one hand, I pretend to stretch the word out of my mouth to hear all the sounds and with the other hand, I write a letter for every sound I hear.*

The topic I'm going to write about today is how cold it is outside. Here is my picture of us having indoor recess. I am going to write two details: "It is cold outside" and "We have to stay inside for recess." Here's how I start: I know how to write those little words "it" and "is" in book writing because we learned them for the Word Wall. Now I need to write the word "cold." I'll put that word "cold" in my mouth like a piece of bubble gum and stretch it out: ccccc-oooo-lllll-dddd. Now, for each new sound that I say, I'm going to write a letter that goes with that sound: /c/ could be a c or a k, but I'm going to guess a /c/ because it starts just like Corey on our name wall. Next, /o/ is easy — it's the letter o saying its name. And /l/ is l like in my name, Lori. And /d/ is the letter d, as in David. Look—when I say all those letters together quickly, they sound like the word cold.

It is cold otsid. We have
to sta insid for reses.

WE DO: Invite the students to "put a word in your mouth and stretch it out." Then have them practice writing individual words in bubble gum writing. Remind students that while "book writing" is the same for everyone, bubble gum writing might look a little different from one writer to another. Compare different renditions of the word "school," for example. The important point is that writers must try very hard to hear all the sounds and use a letter (or letter combination) for every sound that is heard.

YOU DO: *You all know how to write some words in book writing and some words in bubble gum writing. As I visit your writing today, I'm going to ask you to show me the words you wrote using bubble gum writing.* After writing, during Sharing Time, draw attention to some of the words students wrote during Writing Workshop to celebrate their inventive spelling.

Note to Teachers: Generally speaking, I use correct spelling and conventions in my modeled writing. However, if I am demonstrating inventive spelling, I want students to see the process of representing each sound with a letter, and this may not necessarily be the conventional spelling of the word. Some students may try to correct you as you model inventive spelling. Remind them that this is *your* writing; if they know how to write the word in *book writing*, they should do so in their own writing.

Sticky Dot Details

LEARNING GOAL: Students will be able to generate more than one detail about a topic.

I DO: Link this minilesson to your students' understanding of topics and details. Tell them that today they will be adding more than one detail to a topic. *You have become very good at picking a topic to write about and adding a detail. But good writers can usually think of more than one detail about a topic. In fact, sometimes they have lots of details! For example, if my topic is "popcorn," I might add two details like: "It is my favorite snack, and it is white and fluffy like little clouds."*

Place two sticky dots on the back of your hand. Model telling your details before you write them. Tell the students that these dots will help you remember to write one detail for each dot.

I've got lots of ideas for topics in my head right now, but today I'm going to write about the topic "What I did on my summer holidays." Now I need two details. My first detail is "I went camping in the mountains." My second detail is "I saw a bear."

Pre-tell, then write, the first detail. Put one of your sticky dots at the end of the sentence (to signal one detail). Then pre-tell and write the second detail and place the other sticky dot at the end of the sentence, signaling a second detail.

WE DO: Invite students to suggest other details you might add to your writing. Model this strategy by writing one or two additional details and adding sticky dots at the end of each new detail.

YOU DO: Tell students that now it is their turn to choose a topic and write two details about it. Ask them to TTYN (Talk To Your Neighbor) about what two details they're going to write. When they can pre-tell what they are going to write, and it is clear that they understand the concept of two details, give them two sticky dots on the back of their hands. Note that many of your students will pre-tell their details in complete sentences while others will not. For example, a child who chooses a topic such as "My Favorite Foods" might write his/her ideas in a list, such as "pepperoni pizza," "chocolate chip cookies," etc. Others might write: "I went camping. In the mountains. Last summer." Technically, these are each individual details that tell what, where, and when. Both details are acceptable at this point. The objective of this lesson is to generate details, not write complete sentences. Gradually, students can be guided to write complete sentences and replace the dots with periods.

As you circulate around the room and ask each writer to read what he or she has written, ask a few questions and invite each student to tell you more. If the student can add another detail, offer to hand out one more sticky dot!

Adding On Details

LEARNING GOAL: Students will be able to revisit a piece of writing to add details to their picture or text or both.

I DO: Remind students that they already know how to start a new piece of writing. Today, they're going to learn how to add more details to a piece of writing they wrote on a previous day. Show them a piece of your own modeled writing, reminding the students what it says. Then demonstrate and think aloud as you go back and add a detail to the picture or the text or both. For example:

> *This is the piece that I wrote yesterday. I drew a picture of my dog and I wrote: "Maxi is my puppy. She has one floppy ear and one straight ear." You know, I can always go back to that picture and that writing and add more details. There are lots more things I'd like to tell my readers about Maxi. She loves to jump off the dock into the lake. I'm going to draw a picture of the lake behind Maxi and add the detail, "Maxi likes to swim in the lake."*

WE DO: Ask the students to suggest other details you might add to this piece of writing. If time permits, use a shared writing process to add another detail to the picture and to the writing sample.

YOU DO: Tell students that they should go back to a piece of writing they created on another day. They should be encouraged to share their writing with a partner and tell their writing partners what details they might add to the picture or writing. Partners can help by asking questions or giving advice. After pre-telling, students should go ahead and add at least one new detail.

Pushing in Details

All About Shoes

Shoes, shoes, shoes! There are thousands of kinds of shoes. We wear flip flops in the summer and boots in the winter. Skates are for skating. Flippers are for swimming. Galoshes are a kind of boot. Slippers keep your feet warm. And sometimes you wear no shoes at all!

LEARNING GOAL: Students will be able to revise their writing by inserting individual words or brief details.

I DO: *You already know that you can add more details to the end of your writing. But what if you want to add a detail to the middle of your writing? Today you're going to learn to add details by pushing them into a sentence you have already written.* (Put your fingers together to form a point like a caret and make a gesture to simulate pushing with your pointed fingers.)

Use a writing sample like the one shown here to demonstrate how to insert a word or a detail using a caret. Enlarge it on a piece of chart paper or interactive white board to demonstrate the "pushing-in" revision strategy.

Here is an All-About Shoes piece that a student wrote. I think I might push in this detail that elaborates, or gives more information about different kinds of shoes.

WE DO: Invite the students to suggest additional details you might add to the piece and use a shared writing approach to revise the piece.

YOU DO: Have students revisit their completed drafts or drafts in progress in order to find at least two places where they can "push in" a word or a detail.

Shoes, shoes, shoes! There are thousands of ^different kinds of shoes. We wear flip flops in the summer and ^snow boots in the winter. Skates are for skating. Flippers are for swimming. Galoshes are a kind of ^rain boot. and mukluks are a kind of snow boot. Slippers keep your feet warm ^in the house. And sometimes you wear no shoes at all!

The Strikethrough

Pets

Different people like different kinds of pets. Cats are good company, especially when they cuddle up to you and purr. Dogs are fun to play with and take for walks. But some people can't have cats or dogs. Fish, turtles, and birds might make better pets for them. Can you believe some people even have snakes and tarantulas for pets?

LEARNING GOAL: Students will be able to revise or edit their writing by drawing a single line through any text that they wish to delete or change.

I DO: Remind students that Writing Workshop is so grown-up and special that they don't use pencils for writing; instead, they use pens (or skinny markers). Model your own thinking as you wonder: *But what can I do if I change my mind when I'm writing? What if I want to use a different word or a different idea? I can't erase it, so I just have to draw a line through the writing that I want to change and keep on writing! We call that line a "strikethrough." Because I double-spaced my lines, I can just strikethrough the part I want to take out or change and write the new words in the space above. I call that "trading words."*

Demonstrate the use of the strikethrough for the students by modeling a piece of writing, such as the example shown here. *You know, the reason some people can't have cats or dogs as pets is because they're allergic to them. I think I'm going to strike through "can't have" and push in "are allergic to" instead.*

Reinforce the fact that writers are always revising as they write. When you strike through and change something you've written, it's good because it will make the writing better.

WE DO: Use the sample text shown here or another text of your choice to practice using the strikethrough to replace other words or phrases.

YOU DO: Remind students that they can use a strikethrough to change a single word or a group of words. Ask them to try using a strikethrough in their writing today to "trade" a word or group of words.

Stretching the Paper

LEARNING GOAL: Students will be able to add a "stretcher" section to their sheet of paper in order to insert longer details.

I DO: *You already know a lot about revising writing to make it more interesting or clear to a reader. You know about adding details to the end of a piece of writing, using a strikethrough to trade words, and "pushing in" short details in between words. But what if you want to add a bigger chunk of information?*

After I wrote my All-About Healthy Living piece, I decided I should add some more details about some of the ways that people can stay healthy. But I don't have enough room on my sheet of paper to push in all those longer details. What can I do? I wish I could stretch the paper somehow. I know! I can just write my new details on a separate piece of "stretcher" paper. Then I can cut apart my piece of writing where I want the stretcher piece to go, and just tape it right on!

Model for the students how to add the details on a separate piece of paper and cut and paste to insert the "stretcher" into the existing piece (see the sample provided here).

WE DO: Invite the students to suggest another detail you might add to your sample piece of writing, such as describing some healthy foods. Discuss whether this revision would require adding on, pushing in, or stretching the paper. Then make the suggested revisions.

YOU DO: Suggest that students review their previous drafts to find a place that they might stretch the paper to add longer details. You might want to provide them with a prepared writing sample to use.

Healthy Living

The two most important parts of a healthy lifestyle are exercise and good food. People who are active have more energy and stronger bones and muscles. Eating well is another step to good health. Good food and exercise will help you keep fit and enjoy life.

Healthy Living

The two most important parts of a healthy lifestyle are exercise and good food. People who are active have more energy and stronger bones and muscles. There are lots of ways to keep active. Play sports like soccer or dodgeball. Take dance or karate. Walk to school instead of getting a ride. Eating well is another step to good health. Eat plenty of fruits and vegetables. And don't eat too many foods with sugar. Good food and exercise will help you keep fit and enjoy life.

Pruning Your Writing

LEARNING GOAL: Students will be able to revise or edit their writing by deleting unnecessary details.

I DO: *I have a lilac tree in my back yard and one of the things I have to do to look after it is to cut off some branches every year. This cutting is called "pruning" the tree. I don't like having to cut off branches, but I know that the rest of the tree will be stronger and healthier if I remove a few branches each year. Sometimes writing is like that. It's not fun to take out parts of what you've written, but sometimes the rest of the piece of writing will be stronger if you do.*

You know a lot about making writing stronger by adding details or changing details. In this lesson, you're going to learn about making a piece of writing stronger by taking out or "pruning" details.

WE DO: Use the piece of Grade 2 writing on the left or a sample of your choice to talk about which details might be *pruned* to make the writing stronger. For example, this is a piece of writing all about popcorn. Are there any details that are not really about popcorn?

Model "pruning" by drawing a strikethrough to cross out the following detail: "You can also get licorice and candy bars at the movie theater."

YOU DO: Tell students to revisit one of their drafts and look for details that might be pruned to make the piece of writing stronger.

All About Popcorn

Popcorn starts out as hard seeds or kernels. Each kernel contains a small amount of water. When the water is heated up, it turns to steam. The steam makes the kernel explode, turning itself inside out. This makes a delicious snack at the movies and at home. You can also get licorice and candy bars at the movie theater. Popcorn can be a very healthy snack, as long as you don't add too much butter or salt.

All About Popcorn
Popcorn starts out as hard seeds or kernels. Each kernel contains a small amount of water. When the water is heated up, it turns to steam. The steam makes the kernel explode, turning itself inside out. This makes a delicious snack at the movies and at home. ~~You can also get licorice and candy bars at the movie theater.~~ Popcorn can be a very healthy snack, as long as you don't add too much butter or salt.

Editing Your Own Writing

LEARNING GOAL: Students will be able to review their own writing for errors in conventions.

I DO: *We've talked about book writing and sentences and periods and how they can make writing easier for a reader to read. That's why the last thing we do before we publish a piece of writing is try to fix up our words and sentences and punctuation. The big word for fixing up a piece of writing is "editing." Today you're going to learn how to edit your own writing.*

Create a writing sample with a few deliberate errors in spelling, grammar, and punctuation to model a process for students to edit their own writing. Get a special "editing pen." Start by framing the first sentence with your hands. Read the whole sentence aloud to listen for correct grammar, syntax, and word choice. Use the strikethrough or caret to make any necessary corrections, deletions, or additions. Then go back and reread the sentence, this time tapping under every word with your special editing pen. (A skinny marker will leave a small dot under each word, ensuring that no words are omitted or added.) If you come across a word that needs to be written in "book writing," fix it or circle it. (Not all words will need to be spelled conventionally, even in published writing. High-frequency Word Wall words must always be spelled correctly, but student and teacher can decide together which other words should be corrected.)

Repeat this process with each sentence in the writing sample.

WE DO: Provide another sample of written text and use an interactive writing process to have students take turns framing and correcting each sentence.

YOU DO: Give each student an editing pen to practice editing a piece of their own writing or provide a reproduced writing piece for practice.

Keep a collection of brightly colored skinny markers to be used only as editing pens.

How to Edit Your Own Writing
Get a special editing pen.
Read each sentence twice.
First reading:
Read the whole sentence out loud and listen to whether it makes sense to your ear.
Second reading:
Tap every word with your pen as you read it. Circle any words that don't look right and fix any words you know.

Chapter 3   How-To Writing

Procedural text is ubiquitous in today's world. Every time we turn around, we're inundated with instructions, from how to assemble a bookcase to how to return an online purchase to how to get from home to an unfamiliar restaurant. Teaching students about procedures not only helps them navigate this text form, but also supports strategies such as sequencing details, using precise details, and applying a unique grammatical structure—the imperative sentence.

Of the three nonfiction text forms in this book, I prefer to start with How-To writing. It is easy for children to generate ideas and it lends itself to writing several details about a topic.

Many delightful picture books incorporate "How-To" writing into a fictionalized story; these books make entertaining reading, but aren't necessarily useful for understanding the composition and craft of this text form. For teaching procedural writing, look for a typical nonfiction sample with a very basic organizational structure: at the very least, some sort of introduction and a series of steps in chronological order. The *Hands-On Science Fun* series from Capstone Press is a good example, but there are many others. As well, it's easy to come up with real-life examples of the form, such as recipes, online maps, and instructions for games and crafts.

This chapter begins with a minilesson that introduces the structure of the text form. **How to Do How-To Writing** (page 42) takes students through examples of the form in order to analyze the way it is organized and the types of details it includes. Then students are asked to write their own How-To piece; this benchmark writing enables teachers to assess how much students know about the text form and which lessons need to be taught to which students. Based on their assessment, teachers can plan instruction for the whole class as well as small groups. Of course, the lessons in this chapter do not constitute a comprehensive unit. You will want to choose which lessons are appropriate for your students and to supplement instruction from lessons in your own teaching repertoire.

Your students should have no trouble thinking of topics for How-To writing. **Expert Bingo** (page 43) uses a Bingo Card format to encourage students to identify things they're good at doing—and that they can tell others how to do. This lesson uses a Bingo card format to generate topics for writing.

Page	Minilesson Name	Learning Goal Students will be able to…
42	How to Do How-To Writing	…identify the content and structure of procedural writing.
43	Expert Bingo	…generate potential topics for procedural writing.
45	Bossy Sentences	…identify and write imperative sentences.
46	Step by Step	…apply chronological sequence in writing steps in a How-To.
48	Picture It!	…combine illustrations and words to explain how to do something.
49	How Much or What Kind	…use specific quantity or quality details in How-To writing.
50	What Do You Need?	…create an ingredients list as part of How-To writing.
51	Traffic Light Words	…use transition words in How-To writing.
52	Book-End Beginnings and Endings	…introduce and conclude a piece of How-To Writing.

It's a good idea to introduce the imperative sentence right off the bat. Although imperative or command sentences may be found in almost any text form, they are ubiquitous in procedural writing. What makes the imperative sentence unique is the unstated subject of the sentence, the understood "you." Imperative sentences generally begin with verbs, although the verb may be preceded by an adverb, such as *carefully* or *sometimes*. Even Kindergarten writers can understand the concept of imperative or **Bossy Sentences** (page 45), but you may wish to wait to teach the grammatical structure of the sentence until Grade 2 or 3.

When writing procedural text, the order of the steps is just as important as the steps themselves. Many teachers have come up with clever ways of reinforcing chronological sequence, such as following students' instructions for making a baloney sandwich by literally putting a package of baloney on top of a loaf of bread. **Step by Step** (page 46) invites students to collaborate on directions for getting from one place to another in the school—then testing out their own instructions and revising them as needed.

Of course, we want students to know that words aren't the only tool for giving instructions. **Picture It!** (page 48) encourages students to integrate pictures and writing as they tell how to make or do something. Teachers can encourage students to illustrate their How-To steps with hand drawings, but here's a terrific opportunity for students to use digital photography. Your students may already know how to use a tablet, smartphone, or digital camera to take a photograph, but if they do not, it's very easy for them to learn. With some adult assistance, they can take a picture of each step and add it to their writing directions.

In some procedural texts, such as recipes or crafts, the answer to the question **What Do You Need?** (page 50) is as important as what you do. This minilesson teaches students how to create an ingredients list and when it is needed. Both in terms of ingredients and actions, it's essential to use precise and specific language. There's a big difference between taking "several steps" and taking "fifteen steps" or between using "some garlic" and "two cloves of garlic." **How Much or What Kind** (page 49) teaches students to use specific attributes of quantity and quality.

This chapter also offers two minilessons in the writer's craft. **Traffic Light Words** (page 51) such as *first, next,* and *finally* help the writer make transitions from one idea to the next. **Book-End Beginnings and Endings** (page 52) help to hold the whole piece together. Younger students might be taught to write a topic sentence at the beginning to tell the reader what he or she is going to learn. More sophisticated writers open with an explanation of *why* a reader might want to know how to do this activity. Other minilessons on openings and closings include **Start with a Grabber** (page 70), **GO-GO Beginnings** (page 91), and **All-in-All Endings** (page 71); these minilessons are presented in other chapters in this book.

The rubric at the end of this chapter depicts four levels of sophistication in How-To writing, based on the minilessons in the chapter. You might use this checklist as an assessment tool or as an instructional tool for planning lessons for students at different stages of writing development.

From taking prescription medication to paying bills, it's pretty difficult to function in today's world without being able to navigate procedural text. Engaging students in How-To writing sets them on the path to applying this very important but often overlooked text form.

How to Do How-To Writing

Learning Goal: Students will be able to identify the characteristics of the How-To (procedural) text form.

Suggested Literature Link: *How to Make Bubbles* by Erika Shores (Capstone Press, 2011)

I DO: Read aloud at least one good example of a well-structured procedural text, such as *How to Make Bubbles*. If possible, enlarge the text so that students will be able to see the format even if they can't read all the words.

You'll no doubt want to read the book on another occasion and perhaps even try the instructions before revisiting the book during Writing Workshop.

Remember that this is a special kind of book that tells readers how to do something. That's why we call it a "How-To" book.

As you reread the book page by page, invite students to try to identify what the author has done to create this piece of How-To writing. Construct an anchor chart of text features that identify How-To writing, such as the example shown here. *How to Make Bubbles* also includes a scientific explanation, a glossary, an index, and some websites for additional reading. You'll have to decide how many of these text features to introduce to students at the outset.

WE DO: Together, retell how to carry out the procedural steps for whatever text example you used. Reinforce the idea that the steps must be listed in careful, one-at-a-time order. Use a shared writing process to collaboratively create a How-To piece of writing on a topic familiar to everyone, such as "How to Build a Snowman" or "How to Get Ready for Home Time." Be sure to start the piece with a statement of what the reader will learn. End the piece by restating the topic, or what the reader has learned, in slightly different wording.

YOU DO: Briefly generate a small sampling of topics that students might use for How-To writing. Have each student write his or her own How-To writing piece and use these pieces as a benchmark to guide instruction for the rest of the unit.

What Do We Know About How-To Writing?

– It usually starts by telling what the reader is going to learn.
– The writing often tells what materials the reader will need.
– It gives step-by-step instructions telling the reader what to do.
– The instructions might have numbers or words that tell the order of the instructions.
– Sometimes it ends with a review of what the reader has learned to do.

Expert Bingo

Learning Goal: Students will be able to identify good-fit topics for How-To writing.

I DO: Remind students of the characteristics of How-To writing. Tell them that in order to write a strong How-To, they should know quite a bit about the topic. In fact, it's best to choose topics that they're *experts* on.

An expert is someone who knows a lot about something. For example, some of you are experts at skating or bike riding. You're all experts at being in Grade 2! Today, you're going to think about the things you're experts at and those things might just make good-fit topics for How-To writing.

Display the blank **Expert Bingo** card for students (page 44) and fill it in with some of your own examples as you "think-aloud" your reasoning.

SAMPLE EXPERT BINGO CARD

Foods I know how to make	Games I know how to play
Ants on a Log Grilled cheese	Uno Soccer
Activities I know how to do	**Things I know how to make**
ride a bike chicken dance sort the recycling	beaded bracelet folded book
Places I know how to get to	**Silly things I know how to do**
school Southland Mall	Bug my brothers make a bagpipe noise

Make It a Game!

I allow students to shout "Bingo!" when they've completed one item in each box. We keep "playing" or adding topics to the boxes until everyone has had a chance to call "Bingo!"

WE DO: Have students TTYN (Talk To Your Neighbor) about some of the things at which they are experts: hobbies, games, places, etc. (There might be some topics on the sample chart that they are experts at as well.)

YOU DO: Provide each student with an individual Expert Bingo card to complete on his or her own. In order to get a "bingo," they must fill in at least one item (or more for upper grades) in each box. (Kindergarten and Grade 1 writers might be asked to draw a picture in each box.) After completing the chart, invite them to place it in the "topic pocket" of their writing folder to use as a source of writing topics.

Expert Bingo Card

Foods I know how to make:	Games I know how to play:
Activities I know how to do:	Things I know how to make:
Places I know how to get to:	Silly things I know how to do:

Pembroke Publishers © 2015 *Marvelous Minilessons for Teaching Beginning Nonfiction Writing, K-3* by Lori Jamison Rog ISBN 978-1-55138-303-3

Bossy Sentences

Learning Goal: Students will be able to write and understand the structure of imperative sentences.

Suggested Literature Link: *How to Be* by Lisa Brown (HarperCollins, 2006)

I DO: Remind students that when they write a How-To, they tell readers what they need to do in order to make or do something.

In a way, How-To writing sounds a little bit bossy, doesn't it? Do this, make that, go here, stop there! That's why we call the special sentences we use in How-To writing "bossy sentences"—because they tell readers what they need to do. Today we're going to practice reading and writing some bossy sentences.

Revisit the book *How to Be* by Lisa Brown. Remind students that the book tells the reader how to act like different animals. (On the first reading, students often enjoy acting out the behaviors of the animals, as the book intends.) Tell them that on this reading, they should listen for words or groups of words that are bossy; in other words, that tell readers to do something. As you read, pause to discuss the "bossy sentences" encountered. You might record two or three bossy sentences on an anchor chart to revisit after the reading.

In upper primary grades, you've probably taught your students that a sentence must have a *who* or *what* (subject) and an *is* or *does* (predicate). In this case, you might want to point out that bossy sentences deviate from this structure: *Here's a funny thing about bossy sentences. We've been talking a lot about sentences having two parts—a name part (a* who *or a* what*) and a doing part (an* is *or a* does*). But let's take a closer look at those bossy sentences. They only have a doing part! The bossy sentence (also known as a command) is the only kind of sentence without a name part. That's because the name part is understood to be "you"—the reader. For example, in the book, YOU catch fish with your hands; YOU hibernate; and YOU growl. The writer doesn't have to write the word "you" because the reader just knows it. So bossy sentences sound tricky, but they're actually sometimes the easiest kinds of sentences to write. Instead of starting the sentence with a name word, they start with a doing word—a verb:* "catch fish; copy someone; be *curious."*

Review some of the bossy sentences from the Suggested Literature Link above (or from a book of your own choice) and talk about the "bossy words" (verbs) in each sentence.

WE DO: Choose one of the "How to Be" topics in the chart on this page or a similar topic of your own. With the students, create some bossy sentences, using a shared writing process.

YOU DO: Have students create their own "How to Be" books. You might provide a piece of paper folded in four, or staple three or four pages together to encourage students to include several details about their topic. Brainstorm a list of topics from which to choose, such as the list below, but allow students to choose a topic of their own, if they wish. As you circulate around the room, ask students to identify a bossy sentence in their writing and explain why it is a bossy sentence.

Note to Teacher: If you decide to ask students to write a "How to Be" book, take time to model the structure of a multi-page book. Have students sit with a partner and tap each page as they tell what they're going to write on that page.

How to be…				
a bee	a kitten	a teacher	a pencil	a Valentine
a gorilla	a snail	a baby	the moon	a rain forest
a shark	a firetruck	a helicopter	a star	

Step By Step

Learning Goal: Students will be able to write the steps of a procedural text in appropriate sequence.

I DO: Focus on the order (sequence) of the steps as you teach this lesson. *As you know, How-To writing is about following directions or instructions in order to make or do something. Often there are several instructions to follow. We might call those instructions "steps." In almost every piece of How-To writing, it's really important to follow those steps in just the right order. Today, we're going to listen to and follow some real steps—with our feet!—to get from one place to another. This will help us think about putting our instructions in order when we create a How-To piece of writing.*

WE DO: Together, plan a route from the classroom to another place in the school—the office, gym, or library, for instance. With younger students, you may wish to walk along the route and compose the directions as you walk together. (Directions consisting of three steps are enough for Kindergarten students.) Write each step of the directions on a separate piece of paper. (You may wish to remind students that these steps are all examples of "bossy sentences.") Then walk together to follow the directions. Be sure to add or correct any steps that are missing, unclear, or out of order.

Sample Directions Written as Bossy Sentences
1. Go out the classroom door and turn left.
2. Keep walking down the hall until you get to the stairs.
3. Go down the stairs.
4. Turn right.
5. Keep walking until you see the gym door on your left-hand side.
6. Open the gym door and go in.

Talk with the students about the importance of having the steps in the right order. You might want to scramble the sentence strips and have students reassemble them.

What would happen if we followed the mixed-up directions? We wouldn't know where to turn, we'd get lost, and we might never get to where we want to go! That's why putting the steps in the correct order is really important in How-To writing.

YOU DO: Invite students to work individually or in pairs to write the directions to a place they know how to reach, whether on foot or by car. Provide each student with a copy of the Step-by-Step organizer on the next page (or, better yet, teach students how to fold their own piece of paper into four or eight rows). Invite them to write each step of the directions in a separate row. Have them cut up the steps, and reassemble them to ensure that they are in the correct order. Then they can tack or glue down the strips and illustrate each step.

Step-By-Step Organizer

1

2

3

4

5

6

Pembroke Publishers © 2015 *Marvelous Minilessons for Teaching Beginning Nonfiction Writing, K-3* by Lori Jamison Rog ISBN 978-1-55138-303-3

Picture It!

Learning Goal: Students will be able to incorporate illustrations and text to explain the steps in a procedural text.

I DO: Revisit the text presented in *How to Make Bubbles,* or display another text that you have used to point out to students the way the pictures and the writing go together.

Notice that every page has at least one bossy sentence (and sometimes more) as well as a picture to go with it. Often, pictures help the reader understand the directions more clearly. How-To writing might include pictures that are drawn by hand or pictures like these ones that are taken with a camera. As you probably know, these pictures are called photographs.

WE DO: Revisit the route taken in the Step by Step minilesson, but this time use a digital camera, a smartphone, or a tablet to take a photograph of each step. When you return to the classroom, print out or display the photos on a smartboard or LCD projector and combine them with the written directions. Talk with the students about how writers can combine pictures and words to make the directions even easier for a reader to follow.

YOU DO: Have students refer back to one of their previous How-To drafts, or compose a new one, and draw pictures to accompany each step. As an alternative, some classrooms may have the resources to provide digital cameras or tablets to take photographs of each step. (Students will likely need adult support for this activity.)

How Much or What Kind

How to Make A Berry Smoothie

1. Ask a grown-up to help you slice a banana.
2. Put the banana, some frozen berries, some yogurt, and some milk in a blender.
3. Ask a grown-up to help you turn on the blender and blend the mixture until it is smooth.
4. Pour the smoothie into a glass and enjoy!

"Treats on a Log" Alternatives

Lady Bugs on a Log
Cream cheese and dried cranberries

Frogs on a Log
Cheese spread and green grapes cut in half or small pieces of kiwi fruit or green melon

Learning Goal: Students will be able to use precise quantity or quality words in their How-To writing.

I DO: *How many is "some"? Which is more,* many *or* lots? Ask a student to get you "some" books from the bookshelf. Ask another student to get "some" blocks from the block centre. Note whether they bring you the same number of objects. (If they ask, "How many?" even better!) Talk with the students about a problem using words such as *some, a few, lots, many*—we don't always know the exact quantities that these words represent.

Tell students that today they're going to look at a special kind of How-To writing called a *recipe*. A recipe tells readers how to make a certain food. Use the recipe for a berry smoothie, or another recipe of your choice.

Read the recipe aloud. *Here's a How-To for making a berry smoothie. It has bossy sentences, and they're all in the right order. But what's missing? We don't know how many berries or how much yogurt and milk to use. In How-To writing, it's really important to know exactly how much and what kind of each ingredient is needed.*

WE DO: Use an interactive writing approach to revise the recipe to add words that tell "how much." Strike through "some" and replace it with "2 cups (500 mL)" of frozen berries. Insert "1 cup (250 mL)" before yogurt and "1 cup (250 mL)" before milk.

YOU DO: Students can have fun making a healthy treat—and practice their How-To writing. They can make "Ants on a Log" by spreading humus or another type of dip in the hollow of a celery stick (the "log"), then placing raisins on top (the "ants"). There are many different ways to be creative about both the spread and the "creatures." Some alternatives are shown in the box at the left.

You might wish to create an "Ants on a Log" centre for practicing How-To writing. Have students create their own easy-to-make treat, then write out the step-by-step instructions for making their treat. Remind them to be sure to tell "how much or what kind." If an adult supervisor is available, he or she might take photographs of each step to add to the recipe.

What Do You Need?

Learning Goal: Students will be able to create an ingredients list.

I DO: Revisit *How to Make Bubbles* or another literature sample that has an ingredients list. Invite the students to discuss why some How-To writing starts with "What You Need" and how this type of list helps the reader.

Imagine you were trying to follow the directions in How to Make Bubbles, *and suddenly in the middle of your project, you had to run out to the store to buy some dish soap or glycerine. It's always good to have all your materials ready before you start. That's why some How-To writing starts with a list of What You Need.*

Draw students' attention to the list format and talk about how it is different from the way the steps are written. Remind them that the "What You Need" list should always tell specific quantities and qualities—how much and what kind. And here's an opportunity to teach your students a "WOW word": *ingredients.*

WE DO: Talk about the various How-To writing pieces that the students have written and read so far (e.g., how to get from our classroom to the gym and how to make a berry smoothie). Talk about when a piece of writing needs a "What You Need" list and when it doesn't. Together, using a shared or interactive writing approach, create a "What You Need" list for the berry smoothie recipe.

YOU DO: Have students revisit their own How-To writing drafts to find a piece that might require a "What You Need" list. Have them revise their writing by adding the list. They might need to try **Stretching the Paper** (page 36). Otherwise, they have the option of starting a new How-To writing piece that includes an ingredients list.

How to Make A Berry Smoothie
This is what you need:
- 2 cups (500 mL) frozen berries
- 1 cup (250 mL) strawberry yogurt
- 1 banana, sliced
- 1 cup (250 mL) milk
- 1 blender

This is what you do:
1. Ask a grown-up to help you slice the banana.
2. Put all the ingredients in a blender.
3. Ask a grown-up to help you turn on the blender and blend the mixture until it is smooth.
4. Pour the smoothie into a glass and enjoy!

Traffic Light Words

Learning Goal: Students will be able to use transition words in procedural writing.

Suggested Literature Link: *How to Babysit a Grandpa* by Jean Reagan (Knopf, 2012)

I DO: Remind students of previous lessons on the importance of putting steps in the exact order for How-To writing. *Today you're going to learn about special words that help readers understand the order of the steps, words like* first, *and* next, *and* last. *We call these words "traffic light words" because, just like traffic signals, they tell readers when to start, when to keep going, and when to stop.*

WE DO: Revisit a read-aloud such as *How to Babysit a Grandpa.* As you read, have the students listen for "traffic light words" that suggest the order of the steps.

Use a shared writing process to create another silly How-To, such as "How to Look After Your Teacher" (see the example shown here). Number the steps in order as the students provide them.

Invite the students to suggest transition words to replace the numbers in your list. Use sticky notes to add a transition word to the beginning of each sentence:

When we write a How-To writing piece, we can number the steps, the way I did in the sample. But another way to tell the order in which things happen is to use signal words. For example, instead of "number one," we might say, "first." Instead of "number two," what other words might we use? When you get to the last number, invite students to suggest an appropriate word, for example, "finally" or "at last."

Words like first, then, later, *and* finally *act like traffic light signals in writing. They tell us when to get started, in what order to keep going, and when to stop. Words like* first, at the beginning, *and* to start with *are "green light words." They're the "get-started" words. Then there are the yellow light words—the "keep-going" words such as* then, next, later, also, as well, *and* after. *And the red light words, such as* finally *or* last of all *or* at the end *tell readers it's time to stop. You don't always need a traffic light word for every step in your How-To writing, but these words help your reader understand the order of the steps.*

Build an anchor chart of traffic light words. Tell students that they will continue to add to the chart as they discover new traffic light words. Invite students to suggest any other traffic light words they know.

YOU DO: Invite students to write their own How-To pieces, whether silly or serious. Brainstorm a few potential topics, for example, "How to bug your brother or sister" or "How to make your teacher or your mom laugh." Have them practice writing four or five steps featuring traffic light words.

Students should pre-tell what they plan to write by counting the steps on their fingers while explaining to a writing partner what steps they're going to write. Remind students to use a green traffic light word to get started, yellow traffic light words in the middle, and a red traffic light word at the end of their steps. (If you'd like, have them highlight their traffic light words in different colors.)

Revision Tip: Teach students to fold a piece of paper horizontally into eight strips. This provides spaces in which to write each step and facilitates cutting and pasting to reorganize the order of the steps.

How to look after your teacher:

1. Smile at her and tell her she's nice.

2. Dress her warmly for recess.

3. Give her your leftover lunch.

4. Let her get lots of exercise running after you.

5. Make sure she has lots of homework so she doesn't get bored.

Book-End Beginnings and Endings

Learning Goal: Students will be able to write opening and closing sentences for procedural writing.

I DO: Show the students a set of book ends that supports books on a shelf or a table. *Just like these book ends hold together my set of books at both ends, book-end sentences frame my piece of How-To writing at the beginning and at the end.*

Share a piece of How-To writing, such as the example shown here. Invite the students to note that the opening sentence tells what the reader is going to learn how to do in this piece of writing; in this case, to play the card game SNAP!

The closing sentence wraps up the writing piece by telling what the reader has learned or done, in somewhat different words.

WE DO: Collaborate with the students to create book-end beginnings and endings for a sample piece of How-To writing, such as the Berry Smoothie recipe on page 50. For example, you might start with, "Are you feeling hot and thirsty? Here's a treat that's healthy and delicious!" The book end at the end of the piece often reiterates what the reader has done, such as "Take a big sip of your berry smoothie! Don't you feel better already?"

YOU DO: Instruct students to revisit a piece of their own How-To writing that they've already completed and add a book-end beginning and ending.

How to Play SNAP!

SNAP! is a fast-moving card game that's easy to learn. All you need is a deck of cards.

1. Divide the cards evenly among all the players. Each player stacks his/her cards in a pile, face down.
2. Players take turns flipping over the top card in their pile to make another face-up pile.
3. When a player flips a card that matches another card, anyone can shout "SNAP!"
4. The first person who calls "SNAP!" gets both piles of face-up cards.
5. If two people call "SNAP!" at the same time, both piles go into a "pool" in the middle.
6. The game continues in the same way. But everyone watches for a match to the "pool" cards. When there is a match, the first person to shout "SNAP POOL!" gets both piles.
7. If a player shouts "SNAP!" by mistake, then his or her pile goes into the "pool."
8. The player who ends up with all the cards is the winner.

Try it! You'll find that SNAP! is lots of fun for kids and grownups alike.

How-To Writing Rubric

Each level is assumed to also include the criteria from the previous level, even if the criteria are not directly stated.

Level 1	Level 2	Level 3	Level 4
☐ Gives at least three steps in a correct sequence ☐ Uses command sentences	☐ Gives at least three steps in a correct sequence ☐ Uses specific quantity and quality words ☐ Opens with a topic sentence	☐ Gives more than three steps in a correct sequence ☐ Uses specific quantity and quality words ☐ Uses traffic light words to indicate the sequence of steps in a procedure ☐ Opens with a topic sentence	☐ Gives several steps in a correct sequence ☐ Uses specific quantity and quality words ☐ Uses traffic light words to indicate the sequence of steps in a procedure ☐ Uses interesting book-end sentences to open and close the writing piece

Chapter 4   All-About Writing

Informational text is written to inform readers *all about* a particular topic; that's why we call it All-About writing. Unlike narrative text, which is organized chronologically, or by beginning-middle-end, All-About writing is organized around topics and subtopics. For many students, informational text is more difficult to read than fiction, due to challenging vocabulary, dense concept loads, and unfamiliar text structures. But for just as many students (especially boys), nonfiction is the hook that engages them in reading.

There is no shortage of excellent nonfiction mentor texts on topics ranging from aardvarks to zithers. Magazines like *National Geographic Explorer* and *Chickadee* offer a range of articles of interest to youngsters. Browse your school library (or leveled book collection) for nonfiction texts that are short, engaging, and written at an appropriate level for shared reading or read-aloud. (It's not necessary for students to be able to read the complete texts themselves, but it is helpful, even in Kindergarten, to provide an enlarged text that all students can see.) Look for texts that are current, uncluttered by information overload, and written in a friendly, but informational tone. (Many nonfiction texts are written in a narrative voice, which sometimes makes it confusing for young readers learning to distinguish fact from fiction.)

Your students are probably already familiar with informational text, thanks to good teaching and an increasing quality and quantity of nonfiction texts available for children. But even though they may have been taught strategies for *reading* nonfiction, it's possible that your students have never viewed nonfiction from a writer's point of view.

All About All-About Writing (page 59) constructs a framework for the unique features of informational writing. Much informational text today is loaded with visuals and unique text features, such as colorful banners and borders, bold print, text boxes, maps, and tables. It's certainly worthwhile to talk about why the author included all of these features and how they help readers learn all about the topic, but I would start with a fairly traditional, print-based text sample at first, so students can focus on the basic content and organization of the text form. Later, as they prepare to publish their writing, it's a good idea to expose them to a wider range of nonfiction text features. As part of this lesson, students are asked to write an All-About piece on a topic they know well, and teachers can use these

Page	Lesson Name	Learning Goal Students will be able to…
59	All About All-About Writing	…identify the content and organization of informational text.
61	Fact or Fiction?	…distinguish factual information from invented or fictional information.
62	Topic Brainstorm	…brainstorm potential topics for informational writing.
64	Finger Facts	…use their background knowledge to choose appropriate topics for writing.
65	Are/Have/Can Booklets	… generate several facts by subtopic or theme.
66	No More Fuzzy Facts!	…use specific details rather than general details.
67	Telegram Notes	…gather information by taking jot notes.
69	Sticky Facts	… organize their writing by grouping details on the same subtopic together.
70	Start with a Grabber	…open a piece of informational writing with an attention-grabbing sentence.
71	All-in-All Endings	…conclude a piece of informational writing by summarizing the main idea or message.
72	Just-Like Words	…use comparisons to clarify information about a topic.
74	Super Sentences	…use joining words to create more fluent sentences.
75	Labeled Diagrams	…convey information through an illustration that features labels or captions.
76	Same and Different Charts	…compare and contrast information using a chart.

benchmark pieces to assess students' understanding of the text form and to guide instructional planning. The four-level writing rubric at the end of this chapter may be helpful in assessing what students know and can do and what they need to be taught.

One of the earliest things we teach students is that strong writing is all about rich details. But informational writing has a special type of detail—the *fact*. Teaching students to distinguish between factual details and fictional, "made-up" information is challenging, especially when so many texts today combine both fact and fiction. **Fact or Fiction?** (page 61) suggests using a "hybrid" text such as *Diary of a Worm* to provide practice in distinguishing the two genres.

We know that the best topics for informational writing are those that the writer is interested in and knows quite a bit about. **Topic Brainstorm** (page 62) helps writers generate a list of potential topics to write about. **Finger Facts** (page 64) guides writers to identify whether they have enough background knowledge to write an All-About piece on a chosen topic.

The **Are/Have/Can Booklets** structure (page 65) teaches our youngest writers to generate and organize ideas by subtopic. This is a good tool for prompting students to generate a range of details. However, one problem for many young writers is a tendency to use generalities such as "big" or "fast" rather than specific attributes of size or quantity. **No More Fuzzy Facts!** (page 66) reminds students to use specific details that describe the size, speed, or kind of items. You might also find that some students need additional support in using qualifiers such as "some" or "many" versus "all" or "most."

"Are/Have/Can" Lesson: A Teacher's Tale

I often say that in my next life, I want to be one of those teachers who gets everything "right" the first time! As it is, it often takes some trial-and-error to get lessons to work the way I want them to—and even then, I find myself tweaking every lesson to make it suit the particular students I'm teaching. Here is an account of the evolution of my process for taking one lesson from the germ of an idea to what may very well be one of my favorite lessons in the book.

I started with a simple three-column Are/Have/Can graphic organizer, but I found that my young writers needed a lot of one-on-one support to generate more than one fact for each subtopic; plus, the organizer did not allow for accompanying illustrations.

Then I tried creating folded booklets that had two pages for each subtopic, with a sentence stem (i.e., _____ are _____; _____ have _____; _____ can_____) written at the top of each page. Students completed each sentence and added an illustration. It worked fine, but limited my students to two facts on each topic.

Finally, I simply created individual pages with a sentence stem at the top of each page. I started by giving each student one page with each subtopic (i.e., are, have, can) clipped together. I then told them they were going to make their own books, with as many pages as they wanted. After they completed the three assigned pages, they could choose any other pages that they wanted. After the booklets were completed, they could add a cover and—the most exciting part—staple them together!

I required the students to tell me what their new fact was before they were given the additional piece of paper. This requirement proved to be an excellent opportunity for brief individual coaching, reinforcement, and "just-in-time" teaching. And it didn't take long before many students were writing their own sentences, without me providing reproducible sheets with the sentence stems.

Before they stapled their pages, I invited students to consider the best order for their fact pages and to create a cover page. There aren't many lessons that lend themselves to differentiation for students at all stages better than this one!

As early writers start generating more details about a topic, usually by mid-Grade 1, they are likely to do what I call "stream-of-consciousness" writing, in which they record strings of random facts just as they come to mind. **Sticky Facts** (page 69) helps writers think about the topical organization of All-About writing, which entails "sticking" details together that belong together.

At the earliest stages, writers are likely to rely on their background knowledge for All-About writing. At some point, however, we need to encourage them to gather information from outside sources. Taking jot notes is tricky for students of all ages, but it's important to head off plagiarism at the pass. **Telegram Notes** (page 67) uses an analogy to old-fashioned telegrams to teach students about choosing key words to record ideas "borrowed from another writer."

The combined actions of navigating a source of information, selecting relevant facts, and then recording those facts in the form of jot notes are pretty sophisticated tasks for a second- or third-grader. Nonetheless, teaching students to take notes on a topic is a critical skill, especially in this era of "cut-and-paste" from the Internet. That's why it's worth taking time to practice note-taking, whether during Writing Workshop, small-group guided reading time, or other content area studies. As well, you might suggest that students gather only a limited number of new facts on their selected topic, perhaps a maximum of ten, depending on the students.

It can be a challenge to find texts written at an accessible reading level for primary students. For good or ill, the Internet is often the first and easiest source of information for researchers of all ages. Unfortunately, much website reading is too difficult for young readers and may contain advertising or inappropriate content. That means teachers need to take the time to vet websites before students use them for research. And, when all else fails, teachers might even have to create their own web pages or print off documents for students to use as resources.

WWW Wisdom

KidRex.org, Mymunka.com, and Kidzsearch.com are search engines powered by Google, but filtered to keep results appropriate (and safe) for children.

Also, most Wikipedia entries provide a language choice menu on the left, to allow translation from English. One of the options is "Simple English," which brings the reading level down significantly.

Of course the World Wide Web is not the only source of information on a topic. We often find that books and magazines are written at a more accessible reading level for students, especially nonfiction materials from our leveled book collections. And let's not forget human resources; "experts" in the community can be valuable sources of information on a range of topics. A template for **Where I Got My Information** may be found on page 108.

In All-About writing, I generally teach students to focus first on the body of the piece, and then add an opening and closing as "book ends" to hold the piece together. All too many student reports begin with variations of "This report is about..." and close abruptly with "The End." **Start with a Grabber** (page 70) introduces students to two "tricks" for grabbing the reader's attention: with a question or an amazing fact. **All-in-All Endings** (page 71) teaches students to use a summary sentence to wrap up a piece neatly.

Two lessons in this chapter focus on the craft of All-About writing. **Just-Like Words** (page 72) are comparisons, such as similes, that can make information more vivid and interesting to a reader. Often, All-About writing can be full of short, choppy sentences. By using conjunctions such as *and, but, or, because,* and so on, students can create **Super Sentences** (page 74) that flow more smoothly to a reader's ear. Because these lessons ask writers to revise their writing, this might be a good time to revisit **The Strikethrough** (page 35) and **Pushing in Details** (page 34).

And finally, some information is more effectively conveyed visually than in running text. **Same and Different Charts** (page 76) teaches students to present comparative facts in table form. **Labeled Diagrams** (page 75) provides a useful minilesson on how pictures can convey information for writers from Kindergarten to college. The Suggested Literature Link for this lesson is *Scaredy Squirrel* by Melanie Watt. Although they are fictional picture books, the *Scaredy Squir-rel* stories contain examples of many different visual forms, from labeled lists to maps with keys and legends. This lesson can serve as a template for teaching a range of other nonfiction text features, such as:

- Maps (with a key and a legend)
- Illustrated lists
- Headings in different fonts and colors
- Charts and tables
- Cross-sections and "bird's-eye" views
- Graphs (line graphs, bar graphs, and circle graphs, also known as pie charts)
- Infographics (eye-catching combinations of visuals, labels, and numerical information)

As with all the chapters in this book, these minilessons do not constitute a complete unit. Some lessons will be suitable for whole class instruction and others might be more appropriate for small groups. Some of the lesson goals will not be needed by your students at all and others might require extensive repetition and practice before your students achieve mastery. Only you will know which lessons are adaptable to your teaching situation.

Because All-About writing is such a comprehensive text form, I tend to introduce it early in the year just to focus on content and organization. Later in the year, we revisit All-About writing, this time emphasizing text features and the writer's craft as students take a special piece through the publication journey. The final chapter in this book offers additional tips, ideas, and minilessons that can be applied to publishing All-About writing.

The rubric at the end of this chapter depicts four levels of sophistication in All-About writing, based on the minilessons in the chapter. You might use this rubric as an assessment tool or as an instructional tool for planning lessons for students at different stages of writing development.

All About All-About Writing

Learning Goal: Students will be able to identify the structures and features of informational writing.

I DO: Choose a suitable short nonfiction text from your school collection or use the "Frogs in Trouble" sample on page 60. At this point, our goal is to focus on the organization and content of the text form, without too many visuals or subheadings that might distract young writers.

"All-About" writing is written to teach a reader all about a topic. Topics for All-About writing can include almost anything, from asteroids to zebras! The important point to remember is that All-About writing must contain interesting facts about the topic. A fact is a special kind of detail; it is a true piece of information about a topic.

Display and read a passage such as "Frogs in Trouble," which tells *all about* how frogs are disappearing due to changes in the environment. Read one paragraph at a time and discuss which facts the author has included in each section and how those facts belong together. In the sample paragraph, for example, we note that all the facts about *what wetland habitats are* stick together and all the facts about *harming the habitats* also stick together.

Pay particular attention to the first paragraph and the last paragraph. The first paragraph is called the "introduction" because it *introduces* the piece by telling readers what the rest of the writing is going to be about. The last paragraph, or "conclusion," reminds readers of the main message of the piece. You might also note that there are some visuals—a photograph and a map, in this case—that help the reader understand the information in the piece.

Review the characteristics of All-About, or informational, writing with your students. You might wish to create an anchor chart like the one shown here as you and the students identify the features of informational text.

WE DO: Depending on the time expended in analyzing and recording the characteristics of this text form in a chart, you may or may not have time to create a shared-writing report with the students. If you do have time, choose a familiar topic and use a shared writing approach to write a short report that meets the criteria in your anchor chart. You might want to leave this activity for another day, or move right into the independent practice part of the minilesson to assess what your students know about and can do with All-About writing.

YOU DO: Brainstorm some topics of common interest and have students select a topic about which to write a short All-About writing piece. Use these writing samples and the rubric on page 77 as an assessment to guide instructional planning.

What Do We Know About All-About Writing?

- It gives facts about a topic.
- Facts about the same idea or subtopic stick together.
- The introduction tells readers what the piece is going to be about.
- The conclusion summarizes the main message of the piece.
- There are often pictures and other visuals to help readers understand the information.

Frogs in Trouble

 Ribbit! Ribbit! If you've ever heard this sound near a pond or stream, you can bet there are frogs nearby. Frogs live on every continent except Antarctica. But for some reason, there aren't as many frogs as there used to be. In fact, some types of frogs have become extinct. So, why are the frogs disappearing?

Frogs are amphibians. This means they spend part of their lives on the land and part of their lives in the water. Their habitats are wetlands, such as ponds, streams, marshes, and rain forests. Frogs absorb water through their skin. If the water is polluted, therefore, they can get sick or die.

Frogs around the world are being harmed by changes to their habitats. In some places, trees are cut down or swamplands are filled in to build cities and towns. In other places, farmers are using pesticides to get rid of pests that damage their crops.

Scientists are working to save the frogs and their habitats. They know that a healthy habitat for frogs is a healthy habitat for people. And they want us to keep hearing that "Ribbit! Ribbit!" for a long time.

Fact or Fiction?

Learning Goal: Students will be able to distinguish factual writing from fiction or "made-up" ideas.

Suggested Literature Link: *Diary of a Spider* by Doreen Cronin and Harry Bliss (HarperCollins, 2013)

I DO: Revisit a "hybrid" (combination fiction/nonfiction) story such as *Diary of a Spider,* in which facts are integrated into a fictional story.

You'll remember that in this story, some of the details about spiders are true to life, like spiders have eight legs, and some of the details are not real, like spiders can talk. Today you're going to learn about separating true details, which we call "facts," and made-up details, which we call "fiction."

WE DO: Reread the story, and ask students to listen for true details (facts) and made-up details (fiction). Create an anchor chart like the one shown here that lists facts about spiders from the book. (If time permits, you might use these facts to compose a collaborative All-About piece with the students.)

If you think your students need more practice in learning to differentiate factual or informational writing from fiction, play the Fact or Fiction Game. Make a statement (such as "Spiders can talk") and tell students to give a thumbs-up if they think the statement is a fact and a thumbs-down if they think it's made-up, or fiction.

Invite students to tell any other facts they know about spiders.

YOU DO: Tell students that today, in Writing Workshop, they can think of an animal they know about and write four facts about it. Give students a four-square graphic organizer, or teach them to fold a piece of paper in four. Tell them to write one fact about their topic in each square (and make drawings to illustrate the facts, if they wish).

Facts About Spiders

Spiders are not insects because they have eight legs.
Spiders can spin silk.
They move through the air on the silk threads.
They use the silk to make webs to catch small insects for food.
Spiders molt their skin.

How to Make a Four-Square Foldable

1. Fold a piece of paper in half and then in half again.
2. In the corner where two folded edges meet, fold up a little triangle.
3. When the paper is unfolded, it will be in four equal parts with a diamond in the centre.
4. Write the topic in the centre diamond, and then write one fact in each of the four parts. You can illustrate your facts, if you wish.

Topic Brainstorm

Learning Goal: Students will be able to generate potential topics for informational writing.

I DO: *All-About writing can be all about practically anything you want! A good topic for All-About writing is any topic you're interested in, that you already know something about, and that you might like to learn more about. In this minilesson, you're going to create a list of topics that might work for you. Then you'll have some topics in your pocket that you can use for your own All-About writing.*

Display the graphic organizer on page 63 and think aloud as you model for students how you might add two or three topics to each thought bubble. (The topics in the bubbles are based on categories generally appropriate for primary students; feel free to change them to suit your needs.)

WE DO: Invite students to suggest additional ideas for some of the bubbles. Reinforce the idea that a good topic for one writer may not be a good topic for another writer. Remind students that topics should be something they are interested in, that they know something about, and that they might like to learn more about.

YOU DO: Have students TTYN (Talk to Your Neighbor) about some topics that might work for their own All-About writing. Then provide each student with his/her own Topic Brainstorm sheet (see the next page) and guide them as they add two or three ideas to each thought bubble. When everyone is finished, you might choose to give the students another opportunity to talk about some of their ideas with a partner. Have students tuck their Topic Brainstorm sheet into the topic pocket of their writing folders, to access when they need a topic for writing.

Topic Brainstorm Sheet

Finger Facts

Learning Goal: Students will be able to choose appropriate topics for informational writing.

I DO: Remind students about the importance of writers choosing topics they know about and care about. *I was thinking I might like to write an All-About report about boa constrictors. But all I know is that they're very large snakes. So I would have to do a lot of research to make this a good All-About. Maybe it would be better to start with a topic that I know a little bit more about, like dolphins.*

I'm going to use my fingers to count each fact that I already know about dolphins; that's why we call them "finger facts." I know that dolphins are mammals, that they live in the ocean, that dolphin babies are called calves, and that they make noises like clicks and whistles to communicate with each other. When I use my fingers to count these facts, I see I already know four interesting facts about dolphins. I think that's a pretty good start for All-About writing.

WE DO: Invite the students to help you list the facts you already know about a common topic, such as spiders, and count them on your fingers. (By doing this together, you can also help them distinguish a fact from fiction, and discern irrelevant, vague, or repeated facts.) Together, count on your fingers as you state each fact. Talk about how many finger facts make a good starting point for writing, usually three to five. (Of course, students will have an opportunity to brainstorm and research additional facts as they write.)

YOU DO: Have students choose a topic from their Topic Brainstorm sheet and tell a partner at least three finger facts about that topic. If time permits, have students share more than one topic. Then invite students to start a new piece of All-About writing with their chosen topic.

Are/Have/Can Booklets

Polar Bear Facts

*Polar bears **are** Arctic mammals.*
*Polar bears **are** white.*
*Polar bears **have** fat to keep warm.*
*Polar bears **have** two layers of fur.*
*Polar bears **can** swim and dive.*
*Polar bears **can** eat seals.*

Learning Goal: Students will be able to generate several facts by subtopic or theme.

I DO: Remind students that fascinating facts are the most important part of All-About writing. One way to think about facts related to a topic is to think about what the topic *is (are)*, what it *has (have)*, and what it *can* do. Here are some examples of facts on the topic of polar bears.

WE DO: Prepare individual sheets of paper, each featuring one of the following sentence stems:

_____ are _____.

_____ have _____.

_____ can _____.

Choose another familiar topic (animal topics, such as "cats," work well) and invite students to help generate facts about what that topic *is, has,* and *can do*. Record each fact on the appropriate page and illustrate it. (You might choose to have the students do the writing.) As students come up with additional facts, simply add more sheets of paper, writing and illustrating one fact on each page.

This is a good opportunity to distinguish between opinions ("Birds are nice") and facts ("Birds can fly"). As well, you might draw attention to WOW facts, such as "Birds have tail feathers that help them change direction."

YOU DO: Now it's the students' turn to try out the pattern with a topic of their own. Provide each student with three sheets of paper: one with each of the three sentence stems. It's always a good idea to have young writers try out their ideas by telling a partner what they're going to write about before putting their ideas on paper. This will enable everyone to create a minimum three-page booklet. But many of your students will want to add more facts. Prepare additional pages for students to choose from as they generate more facts on their topics. (Ultimately, even Kindergarten students should be able to record the facts on their own, without a sentence stem to complete.) Some students will stop at three or four pages; others will complete several more. When they're finished, students can be helped to add a cover, organize their pages, and staple the booklets together.

No More Fuzzy Facts!

Learning Goal: Students will be able to use specific facts and numbers rather than general terms.

I DO: *When I read All-About writing, it's not enough for me to know that "a hippo is big" or that there are "lots of kinds of spiders." Readers want to know* how big *the hippo is or* how many *kinds of spiders there are. We* call words like "big" or "lots" fuzzy facts *because they're not exact. Today, you're going to learn about replacing fuzzy facts with exact facts.*

Turtles

Some turtles are big. Some turtles are small. Turtles can swim. Turtles can eat. Most turtles live outdoors. Turtles can get very old.

WE DO: Display the All-About writing piece about turtles shown here. Ask students to identify some fuzzy facts, such as "Some turtles are big. Some turtles are small." Then talk about how they can change those fuzzy facts into exact facts. Also, facts like "Turtles eat" or "Most turtles live outdoors" are also fuzzy facts because they don't tell us specifically what turtles eat or exactly where they live in the outdoors. Together with the students, revise the piece to replace fuzzy facts with exact details.

Remind students that sometimes even grown-up writers don't know the exact facts and they need to look at a book or website to find out.

YOU DO: Suggest that students review their own writing to look for fuzzy facts. Remind them that fuzzy facts are facts that seem to ask for more information, such as *how much* or *what kind*. They should revise any fuzzy facts by changing or inserting specific information to replace imprecise details. As they do future writing, they need to be aware of avoiding fuzzy facts and using specific details instead.

Telegram Notes

Learning Goal: Students will be able to use jot notes to gather information for writing.

I DO: *Even when writers choose topics that they know something about, they often need to learn some more in order to write all about the topic. Finding out about a topic is called research. Writers do research by gathering facts from books or magazines or websites or even other people. But we don't just copy exactly every word that another writer says. We borrow just enough words from that writer to help us remember the facts or details.*

Back in the olden days, before there was texting or even e-mail, people had discovered other ways to get a message quickly to other people who were far away. One way was called a telegram—a message communicated by an operator using a device called a telegraph set to send out signals a long distance along a wire. Telegrams were very expensive and every single word cost money. So you wanted to make sure you didn't use any words that you didn't need. You tried to make your message clear by using as few words as possible.

That's similar to what we do when we get facts from another writer. We capture the key ideas using as few of the other writer's words as possible.

Read the text below together and have students TTYN (Talk to Your Neighbor) about what facts they learn about chocolate.

> People have enjoyed chocolate for thousands of years. It was first used in a spicy drink. Then people figured out to add sugar instead of chili peppers. And the world fell in love with chocolate. Today there are over 30,000 kinds of chocolate candies. And there is even chocolate toothpaste, chocolate pasta, and chocolate soap! No wonder it's the world's favorite flavor!

Let's look at the first sentence. If I want to make a note about this fact without borrowing too many of the writer's words, what might I say? If I just say, "thousands of years," will I remember that's how long people have been enjoying chocolate? I'm going to write that fact down with a little dash or a little dot in front of it, to show that it's a telegram note and not a complete sentence.

WE DO: Together with the students, create a bulleted list of facts about chocolate like the one above. Then have students TTYN (Talk to Your Neighbor) about what they remember about chocolate, using only the telegram notes as a guide. This will indicate to the students whether the telegram notes provided enough information to recall the complete fact.

Provide the students with additional paragraphs to practice taking telegram notes. (A sample text on Penguins is provided on page 68.) This is a very difficult concept and most students need plenty of guided practice before they will be able to take their own notes effectively.

YOU DO: Invite students to choose a topic of their own and begin to gather telegram notes from a resource of their choice. (Teachers may want to approve the resource in advance.)

Telegram Notes About Chocolate

- Thousands of years
- Spicy drink
- Add sugar instead of chili peppers
- 30,000 kinds of candies
- toothpaste, pasta, soap
- world's favorite flavor

Where I Got My Information
Page 108 is a reproducible template for recording title, author, and copyright information for various sources.

Penguins

Penguins can't fly but they can move in other ways. Instead of wings, they have flippers that help them swim. On land, the penguins use their tails and flippers to help them balance. Penguins either waddle on their feet or slide on their bellies across the snow. This is called "tobogganning."

The female penguin lays the egg, then she goes off to find food for the baby. The male takes care of the egg while she is gone. The male holds the egg on his feet and tucks it under his feathers to keep it warm until it hatches. When the female comes back, they take turns looking after the chick.

Sticky Facts

All About Bees

Bees can make honey. Worker bees feed the queen. Bees dance to communicate. The queen lays the eggs. Bees have five eyes. Worker bees are all girls and drones are all boys. Drones don't have stingers. Bees have two sets of wings.

Learning Goal: Students will be able to organize their writing by grouping details on the same subtopic together.

I DO: Rich, informative details are the heart of All-About writing. But the order in which those details are written is also important. *Let's take a look at this Grade 1 student's report about bees. There are lots of interesting details all about bees, but they jump all over the place. There's something about what bees can do at the beginning and at the end. There's something about different kinds of bees at the beginning and at the end. It's much easier for a reader to understand a terrific All-About like this if we stick details together that belong with one another.*

> There are different ways to reorganize this text. Here is one option:
> *Bees can make honey. They dance to communicate. Bees have five eyes and two sets of wings. Worker bees are all girls and drones are all boys. Drones don't have stingers. Worker bees feed the queen. The queen lays the eggs.*

WE DO: Together with the students, look for facts in the sample piece that should "stick together." Have students take turns highlighting in one color all the facts that tell what bees do. Then have them highlight in another color facts about different kinds of bees. There are two possible techniques for reorganizing the report: either rewrite it in a more appropriate order or literally cut the sentences apart and glue them back together.

YOU DO: Tell students to read over the All-About writing that they have done and have them ask themselves: *Did you stick the details together that belong together? Do you need to move some of your details to another place?* Students might reorganize an existing draft or create a new draft, ensuring that details on the same subtopics are "stuck together."

Start with a Grabber

Learning Goal: Students will be able to write engaging leads for informational writing using a question or an amazing fact.

Two good ways to **grab** your reader:
– A question
– An amazing fact

I DO: Remind students of previous discussions about the importance of leads that grab a reader's attention. The very first sentence of a piece of writing will make readers decide whether they are interested in reading the rest of the piece. *Writers try to "grab" their readers with a lead that makes the reader want to read more. Today you're going to learn two ways to grab readers and make them want to read your All-About writing.*

Revisit the All-About chocolate piece on page 67. Read the first sentence together: "People have enjoyed chocolate for thousands of years." The writer has tried to grab our attention with an interesting fact. Another way to open that piece might be with a question, such as: "What's the world's favorite flavor? If you guessed chocolate, you are right!"

Tip for Writers

Words like *interesting, unusual, fascinating, amazing, strange, mysterious,* or *odd* often grab a reader's attention.

WE DO: Use any of the nonfiction sample texts in this chapter to collaborate on an opening sentence that grabs the reader's attention. For example, "Penguins" on page 68 might open with an interesting fact such as, "Penguins are different from any other birds on earth" or "Penguins have some unusual ways of getting around." Another option is to use a question. Sometimes we can combine an interesting fact with a question by starting with "Did you know…?" or asking a question such as "What's the only bird that would rather swim than fly?"

YOU DO: Have students revisit one of their pieces of All-About writing—a completed draft or a work in progress—to add a more engaging lead that includes a question and/or an amazing fact. Suggest that they try to write a few different leads and consult a writing partner to see which lead might do a better job of grabbing a reader's attention.

All-in-All Endings

Learning Goal: Students will be able to write a summary sentence to wrap up (conclude) a piece of informational writing.

I DO: *A good ending is like the bow on a present; it just wraps the piece up neatly. One kind of ending is an "All-in-All" ending. It says, "All in all, this is what the writing is about." Look at the All-About piece of writing on chocolate (page 67). It starts with a hook—an amazing fact—and ends with an "all-in-all" statement—the main message of the piece. The whole piece of writing is about how people all over the world love chocolate. The last sentence doesn't say "all in all," but you can hear it in your mind as you read.*

WE DO: Look at the "All About Bees" report on page 69 or choose another piece of informational text that lacks a conclusion.

Let's take a look at this report titled "All About Bees." What was the main message that the writer is trying to tell us? We might say, "All in all, bees have some very unusual habits" or even "All in all, bees are busy creatures. No wonder people say, 'Busy as a bee'!" We don't always have to use the words "all in all" in our endings, but it's useful to say those words in our heads as we write an ending.

The chart shown here suggests some phrases that writers might use for constructing "all-in-all" statements.

YOU DO: Have students revise a piece of All-About writing by adding an "All-in-All" ending.

Some words to use for All-in-All Endings

- All in all,…
- As you can see,…
- And so…
- It's clear that,…
- In conclusion,…
- To sum up,…

Just-Like Words

Learning Goal: Students will be able to use comparisons, including similes, in their written descriptions.

Suggested Literature Link: *Big Blue Whale* (by Nicola Davies, Candlewick, 1997) (You can find a reading of this book at https://vimeo.com/60259773.)

I DO: Use a chart or interactive whiteboard to display this excerpt from *Big Blue Whale* or another nonfiction text of your choice:

> ***Reach out and touch the blue whale's skin. It's as springy and smooth as a hard-boiled egg, and it's as slippery as wet soap. Look into its eye. It's as big as a teacup and as dark as the deep blue sea.***

Talk about what the author has done to help readers understand information about the blue whale. *Do you have a better understanding of how big the whale's eye is when the author compares it to the size of a teacup? When a writer compares a detail about the topic to something else the reader is likely to know about, we call that "just-like" writing. The blue whale's skin feels hard and smooth just like an egg, but it's slippery just like soap. You probably have never felt a blue whale's skin, but you've probably felt an egg and slippery soap. By using a "just-like" comparison, the author helps you understand what the blue whale's skin feels like.*

Just-like words compare something you might not know about to something you probably do know about to help you understand a topic better.

WE DO: Talk with the students about how writers use "just-like" words to describe other topics. Notice that writers try to use interesting and unusual words and ideas for "just-like" comparisons. For example, a writer might describe a coin as being as round as a circle or a ball, but that's pretty ordinary. To say it's as round as a full moon or as round as an owl's eye would be much more interesting.

Choose a common object, such as a button, a pinecone, or a flower. Talk about how we can compare this item with other items, using sentence stems such as:

- It's as big/small/light/heavy as…
- Its color is like…
- Its shape is as _____ as a _____.
- It feels like a _____.

If you think your students need more practice writing interesting similes, provide them with the graphic organizer on page 73 and invite them to work in pairs or small groups. Have them choose a familiar object such as a coin, pine cone, or feather and write a Just-Like piece of writing using as many rows in the organizer as they find appropriate—and then have classmates guess what they're describing.

YOU DO: Have students revise a piece of their All-About writing to insert at least one "just-like" comparison.

Just-Like Riddles

Can you guess what I'm describing?

Characteristic	Just-Like Comparison
Color	
Shape	
Size	
Weight	
Texture	
Smell	
Sound	

Pembroke Publishers © 2015 *Marvelous Minilessons for Teaching Beginning Nonfiction Writing, K-3* by Lori Jamison Rog ISBN 978-1-55138-303-3

Super Sentences

Learning Goal: Students will be able to combine sentences to make them more interesting and rhythmical.

I DO: Share the All-About writing piece titled "How Penguins Move" in the box shown here. (You might even read it aloud in a choppy voice to emphasize its lack of fluency.) *This writing tells some interesting facts all about how penguins move. But the writing sounds a bit choppy to the ear because it has lots of short sentences. Sometimes we can join up shorter sentences to make them sound more flowing to a reader's ear. That makes a Super Sentence, because it's two sentences combined into one. For example, we might add the word "because" to join up the first two sentences to make the Super Sentence: "Penguins can't fly because they don't have wings."*

WE DO: Invite the students to find two other sentences that might be joined together to make a Super Sentence. For example, "They waddle on their feet" and "They slide on their bellies" might be joined with *and* or *or*. Show students the necessary revisions. This is a good time to slip in a little editing, as you have to delete a period and replace a capital letter with a small letter when you join the two sentences together. Now read the piece aloud together to hear how much more smoothly the sentences flow.

Make and display an anchor chart of joining words, such as the one shown here. Keep it alive by adding new joining words as your students discover them.

YOU DO: Invite students to reread one of their own pieces of writing to listen for choppy sentences that could be joined together to make Super Sentences. Suggest that they highlight the joining words that they use.

How Penguins Move

Penguins can't fly. They don't have wings. They have flippers to help them swim. They waddle on their feet. They slide on their bellies. This is called tobogganing.

Some Joining Words

and
because
or
but
so
although
as

Labeled Diagrams

Learning Goal: Students will be able to convey information through an illustration that features labels or captions.

Suggested Literature Link: *Scaredy Squirrel Makes a Friend* by Melanie Watt (Kids Can Press, 2011)

I DO: An Internet search will turn up literally hundreds of examples of labeled diagrams, from the human eye to a starfish to a Lego construction. Although the *Scaredy Squirrel* books are fictional, they contain many different text features useful for informational writing, from maps with legends to illustrated lists. Revisit this text to look specifically at labeled diagrams. Note that the author Melanie Watt has combined words and pictures to give us some information about topics such as the perfect friend (and the not-so-perfect friend) for Scaredy. *A diagram is a special kind of illustration used to teach a reader about a topic. The words that the author uses to describe different parts of the diagram are called "labels." Just as the label on a can of soup or a jar of jam gives you information about what's inside the product, a label on a diagram gives you more information about what the diagram shows.*

Together, read the pictures and the words and discuss ways in which the labeled diagrams sometimes give information that's not in the text, and sometimes clarify information that's in the text as well.

WE DO: Choose a topic such as an animal and sketch (or have a student sketch) a diagram of it on a sheet of chart paper. Use an interactive writing approach to take turns adding labels to the diagram.

YOU DO: Tell students that they will be expected to include a labeled diagram in their All-About writing. Encourage them to experiment with labeled diagrams as they work on their various writing projects.

Same and Different Charts

Learning Goal: Students will be able to use a chart or table to compare and contrast facts about similar topics.

I DO: Show an example of a comparison chart such as the one below or another of your choice. *Sometimes All-About writing looks like paragraphs and sometimes it takes the form of pictures or labeled diagrams. But there are other ways to write all about a topic. We can use a chart like this when we want to tell about details that are the same and different about two or three or more different topics.* Clarify that we use Same and Different Charts for topics that have some things in common and some things that are different. In the example below, all the topics are Sports and they all involve ways of playing, ways of scoring, and equipment that must be worn.

Take time to model and explain how to read a comparison chart.

	SOCCER	HOCKEY	BASEBALL
Basic equipment	Ball	Puck and stick	Ball and bat
How to score	Kick the ball into a large net.	Use a stick to shoot the puck into a small net.	Hit the ball and run around three bases.
Where to play	Large field called a pitch	Large ice rink	Large field called a diamond with three bases and a home base
Safety equipment	Very little padding or protection except sometimes shin guards	Lots of padding and protection, helmets, gloves, masks for goalies	Glove, batting helmet

WE DO: Ask the students to TTYN (Talk to Your Neighbor) to review the features of a Same and Different Chart and how it can be used for All-About writing. Choose a pair of familiar topics and use a shared writing process to create a collaborative chart or have students work in pairs to create their own comparison charts. For example, you might create a chart comparing and contrasting two or more seasons, such as summer and winter. Subtopics might include: What We See, What We Do, and What We Wear.

You Do: Have students review their own All-About writing topics and select one that lends itself to creating a Same and Different Chart.

All-About Writing Rubric

Each level is assumed to also include the criteria from the previous level, even if the criteria are not directly stated.

Level 1	Level 2	Level 3	Level 4
☐ Contains at least two or three facts that stick to a topic ☐ Includes an illustration or a labeled diagram	☐ Opens by introducing the topic ☐ Contains at least three details about the topic ☐ Uses some specific quality and quantity words ☐ Includes a visual such as a labeled diagram	☐ Opens with a hook to grab the reader's attention ☐ Contains several interesting facts about the topic ☐ Begins to show evidence of research beyond background knowledge ☐ Begins to organize details by subtopic ☐ Uses a visual such as a labeled diagram to enhance or add information ☐ Wraps up with an ending sentence	☐ Opens with a hook to grab the reader's attention and introduce the topic ☐ Includes many interesting facts gleaned from research and background knowledge ☐ Organizes details by subtopic ☐ Uses specific quantity words and qualifiers (e.g., some, all, most) ☐ Includes at least one Just-Like comparison ☐ Concludes with an All-in-All statement that summarizes the main point ☐ Records sources of information

Chapter 5   I-Think Writing

Our beginning writers are no strangers to persuasion. Every time they beg their parents to order pizza for dinner or to extend their bedtime, they're using their powers of persuasion. Our job is to guide them in transferring their persuasive skills to the printed page. That's what "I-Think" writing, or opinion writing, is all about.

Opinion writing helps young writers articulate their thinking, build reasoning skills, and develop logical and rational support for their ideas. It guides them in understanding that others may have different points of view from their own. And it provides a forum for authentic writing about topics that matter to them.

This chapter comprises a set of minilessons related to the composition and craft of opinion or "I-Think" writing, starting with an introduction to the text form in **What's I-Think Writing?** (page 81).There are many delightful picture books that exemplify the art of persuasion (such as the list of titles on this page); however, when introducing the structure of I-Think writing, it's more useful to present a more traditional nonfiction format, such as the example on page 81. After the introductory lesson, ask the students to write their own I-Think pieces independently. You'll be able to assess these pieces to see what your students already know about opinion writing and you can plan your instruction from there.

It may be obvious from your assessments that some of your students don't understand what an opinion is. **What's an Opinion?** (page 82) helps distinguish an "I-know" (a fact that is generally accepted to be true) from an "I-think" (something that only some people believe to be true).

Effective opinion writing has a strong voice and conveys the writer's passion for the topic. That's why students need to find topics that matter to them. The **Love It or Loathe It** minilesson and chart (page 83) help generate a list of themes and ideas that each writer feels strongly about and that could serve as topics for writing.

Students of all ages are fairly skilled at stating their opinions, but are not always as adept at supporting those opinions. **Adding a "Because"** (page 84) reminds even beginning writers that their opinions will carry more weight if they provide reasons for those opinions. As a structure for organizing opinion writing, the **OREO Organizer** (page 86) demands some fairly sophisticated thinking on the

Page	Lesson Name	Learning Goal Students will be able to…
81	What's I-Think Writing?	…identify the features of opinion writing.
82	What's an Opinion?	…distinguish a fact from an opinion.
83	Love It or Loathe It	…choose their own topics for opinion writing.
84	Adding a "Because"	…provide reasons to support their opinions.
86	OREO Organizer	…plan a piece of opinion writing by stating the opinion, offering reasons and explanations to support their opinion, and restating the opinion.
88	Convince Your Reader	…consider audience and purpose when writing a piece of persuasive writing.
91	GO-GO Beginnings	…open a piece of persuasive writing with a hook and an opinion.
92	Wraparound Endings	…conclude a piece of persuasive writing by restating their opinion.
93	Shouting Sentences	…understand and apply exclamatory sentences.
95	The Magic of Three	…use three parallel words or phrases to add voice and rhythm to opinion writing.

part of young writers. It asks writers to not only state an opinion and give reasons for that opinion, but also to explain their reasoning with examples, evidence, and other elaboration.

Persuasive or argumentative writing takes I-Think writing to a higher level by considering audience and purpose. It's not just about what "I think"; it's more like "I-Think-and-I-Want-You-to-Think-the-Same." **Convince Your Reader** (page 88) teaches students about planning their writing with audience and purpose in mind. Although this minilesson only takes writers through the planning stage of the writing process, it can be the first step of the process of planning, drafting, revising, and even publishing a piece of writing.

At first, we ask young writers to organize I-Think writing simply by stating an opinion and offering reasons for that opinion. However, as writers become more sophisticated, we can teach them to add an engaging introduction, as in **GO-GO Beginnings** (page 91) and to conclude the piece by restating their opinion in a slightly different way, as in **Wraparound Endings** (page 92).

Finally, in this chapter, we look at two elements of the writer's craft often found in I-Think writing. Exclamations or **Shouting Sentences** (page 93) convey strong feelings about an idea and add voice and passion to a piece of writing. **The**

Magic of Three (page 95) demonstrates an interesting and sophisticated grammatical structure that lends rhythm and voice to a piece of writing. This structure involves listing three parallel words, phrases, or sentences that convey or support an idea. This technique (known as a tricolon in grown-up grammar) can serve as a powerful persuasive tool. In fact, U.S. President Barack Obama's inaugural speech used this technique 22 times!

As with other chapters in this book, the ten minilessons on I-Think writing in this chapter offer a smorgasbord of ideas from which to choose. Teachers are encouraged to select and adapt these lesson ideas in order to meet the specific needs of their students.

What's I-Think Writing?

Learning Goal: Students will be able to identify the features of opinion writing.

I DO: Explain to your students that they're going to be learning about a new kind of writing that doesn't just give information about a topic, but that also tells what the writer *thinks* about the topic.

When we tell whether we like something or don't like something, whether we think something is funny or beautiful or scary, we're giving an **opinion** *about it. I-Think writing is all about offering your opinion on a topic.* Show students the writing sample below, or another sample of your choice and read it together.

We Need More Books!

I think we need more books in our classroom library. Most of the students have read most of the books. And not everyone is interested in every book. There just aren't enough books for a whole year. Lots of the books are in bad shape. They've been read over and over again until they're falling apart. It's important for kids to read a lot. So we need to make sure there are a lot of books for them to read.

What Do We Know About I-Think Writing?

- It gives an opinion about a topic—how the writer feels or thinks.
- The writer gives several reasons for his or her opinion.
- It often begins and ends with the opinion, sometimes using words that are a bit different.
- It often uses the words I, we, or you.

Tell the students, or elicit from them, a description of the structure of this text form, which consists of an opinion, some reasons that elaborate on that opinion, and a restatement of the opinion. Note that there's no magic number of reasons; quality is more important than quantity. (That being said, encourage students to provide at least two good reasons.)

WE DO: Use a shared writing approach to collaboratively compose a We-Think piece on a common topic such as "Grade 2 is the best grade."

YOU DO: Generate a small number of potential topics with students and invite them to write their own I-Think writing pieces. Use these pieces to assess what students can demonstrate about opinion writing and plan future instruction accordingly.

What's an Opinion?

Learning Goal: Students will be able to distinguish between an opinion and a fact.

Suggested Literature Link: *Duck! Rabbit!* by Amy Krouse Rosenthal (Chronicle Books, 2009). (You can find a YouTube video of this book posted by the publisher at www.youtube.com/watch?v=hPCoe-6RRks.)

I DO: Explain to students the difference between an opinion and a fact. *An "opinion" is something you believe, something that might or might not be based on facts and that might or might not be the same as another person's opinion. For example, one person's opinion might be that spring is the best season and another person's opinion might be that fall is the best season. Neither person is wrong, because that's what they think or believe. It's their opinion. On the other hand, if you say spring is the season that comes after winter, that's a fact. It's true for everybody. Today you're going to have a chance to think a little more about the difference between a fact—a true detail—and an opinion—what someone thinks or believes about a topic.*

Read the book **Duck! Rabbit!** to the students. Look at the cover and ask the students for their opinions: *How many of you believe that this is a picture of a rabbit on the cover? Your **opinion** is that it's a rabbit. How many of you believe that this is a picture of a duck? It's your **opinion** that the picture is a duck. Listen for the different reasons for the different opinions in this book.*

Read the whole book, reminding students of the meaning of the word *opinion* and that there are different reasons for someone's opinion.

You may wish to reinforce the difference between opinions and facts with information such as:

- A fact is something that has actually happened or is happening now or is known by everyone to be real or true. A fact can be supported with evidence.
- An opinion is something that some people believe exists or happens or is true, but that may not be true for everyone or even real. An opinion often cannot be proven.

WE DO: Play a "Fact or Opinion?" game. Read a series of statements aloud and have students give a "thumbs-up" in response to factual statements and make an "O" with their thumb and forefinger in response to opinions.

- Bananas are the tastiest fruit.
- Blue whales are the largest mammals.
- Soccer is more fun than hockey.
- Vanilla is the best flavor of ice cream.
- The days are longer in summer than in winter.
- Our school is on _____ Street.

YOU DO: Kindergarten and Grade 1 students might create their own "My Opinion" books. You may wish to provide a series of sentence stems from which to choose, for example, "I think the best toy/game/food/color/place to go on vacation is…," etc. Some students should be expected to provide a reason as well. On each page, the students will write one sentence and illustrate it. They can write as many pages as they want and staple them together into a booklet.

Love It or Loathe It

Learning Goal: Students will be able to identify topics that they feel strongly about as potential topics for writing an opinion piece.

I DO: Tell students that one kind of opinion is to think of "the best" or "the worst." (The word "loathe" is a WOW word that means the same as "dislike a lot.") In this minilesson, students will learn how things we love and things we loathe can make great topics for opinion writing.

Model for the students how to complete a "Love It or Loathe It" T-chart in which the first column is headed "Love It!" and the second column is headed "Loathe It!" As you list two or three items for each column of the chart, briefly explain to students why you've added those words to the list.

WE DO: Use a guided writing approach to provide scaffolding for students as they complete their own T-charts. Have students simply fold a piece of paper in half to create two columns and label the two columns "LOVE" and "LOATHE." Tell them to list three or four (or more) things they *love* on the left side of the chart and three or four things they *loathe* on the right side. For younger students in Kindergarten and Grade 1, you might choose to divide or fold a piece of paper in four sections and have them draw-and-write two things they love and two things they loathe. After providing time for students to complete their "Love It or Loathe It" charts, invite them to TTYN (Talk to Your Neighbor) about the ideas on their charts.

YOU DO: Have students tuck their charts into the topic pockets of their writing folders to use as topics for writing opinion pieces.

Adding a "Because"

Learning Goal: Students will be able to give reasons and explanations for their opinions.

Suggested Literature Link: *Would You Rather?* by John Burningham (Red Fox, 1994)

I DO: Remind students that an opinion is something you believe or you think, but that one person's opinion might be different from someone else's opinion. Nevertheless, it's important to provide a reason or reasons for your opinion. In fact, good I-Think writing always gives at least one—and sometimes more—reasons for the opinion. In today's lesson, students will practice adding "because" to their opinions.

Revisit selected pages from the picture book *Would You Rather?* or use the reproducible cards on page 85. Read aloud one of the "Would you rather…?" choices and model for the students which option you would choose and the reasons for your choice. Make sure to be very clear about which part is the opinion and which part is the reasoning.

WE DO: Ask another "Would you rather…?" question and have students TTYN (Talk to Your Neighbor) about their choices and reasons for their choices. Continue the process until you are confident that students understand the concept of adding a because, or reason, for their opinions. Encourage students to give as many reasons as they can.

YOU DO: In Writing Workshop, students should be expected to practice writing opinions and reasons to back up those opinions. Students could either select a "Would you rather…?" card at random and write a response, or choose a topic from their "Love It or Loathe It" T-chart.

Remind students to think of as many reasons as they can to support their opinions.

Sometimes it helps to reinforce separating the opinion from the reasons by using gestures. For example, one of the American Sign Language hand signs for "because" is to touch one's forehead with four fingers, then swoop the fingers into a fist with a thumb up. (http://www.handspeak.com) Invite students to state an opinion, then use the hand sign for "because" as they state the reason.

Would You Rather...?

Would you rather have the superpower to be invisible or to fly?	Would you rather have a shark in your bathtub or an elephant in your closet?
Would you rather be super strong or super fast?	Would you rather eat chocolate ants or alligator ice cream?
Would you rather have all-day recess or all-day gym?	Would you rather face a dinosaur or a gorilla?
Would you rather hunt for treasure buried in the ground or in a shipwreck at the bottom of the ocean?	Would you rather get up really early in the morning or stay up really late at night?

Pembroke Publishers © 2015 *Marvelous Minilessons for Teaching Beginning Nonfiction Writing, K–3* by Lori Jamison Rog ISBN 978-1-55138-303-3

OREO Organizer

OREO Organizer

O = Opinion
R = Reasons
E = Explanation
O = Opinion

Learning Goal: Students will be able to organize a piece of persuasive writing that expresses an opinion, reasons for the opinion, and an explanation of their reasoning.

I DO: Remind students of the structure of I-Think writing: state an opinion, give reasons to support your opinion, and then restate the opinion. *You know that it's important to give reasons to support your opinions. But if you want to make your I-Think writing even more powerful, you need to **elaborate** on your reasons. Remember that **elaborating** means adding more details, like explaining or giving an example.*

*I like to think of the word OREO to remind me of how to organize I-Think writing. Think of your statement of your **opinion** as the cookie on the top. The icing in the middle is made up of the **reasons** for your opinion and the **explanations** for those reasons. An explanation might include some examples, facts, or further elaboration. Then you restate your **opinion** at the end, which is like the cookie on the bottom.*

Here's Hayden's OREO organizer explaining why he thinks Lego is the world's best toy.

O: I think Lego is the best toy in the world.	
R: There are kits and instructions to make amazing creations.	**R:** You can easily make super-cool creations from your own imagination.
E: I could follow the instructions to make the Death Star—which was the second biggest Lego set in the world!	**E:** Lego has over 2000 different sizes and shapes and colors. You can make anything you can imagine. You can take the pieces apart and start all over again to make something new.
O: That's why kids all over the world love Lego.	

WE DO: Enlarge the OREO planning template and use a shared writing approach to practice completing an OREO organizer on a topic of common interest, such as, "Recess should be longer."

YOU DO: Have students choose an opinion from their "Love It or Loathe It" T-charts or select another topic of their choice to complete an OREO organizer. They should come up with at least two valid and sensible reasons for their opinion—and they may add more reasons if they wish.

Note to Teachers: This organizer is an excellent foundation for supporting ideas in I-Think writing. Have students practice completing at least two or three organizers before choosing one topic to turn into a draft.

OREO ORGANIZER Template

O:

R: R:

E: E:

O:

Pembroke Publishers © 2015 *Marvelous Minilessons for Teaching Beginning Nonfiction Writing, K-3* by Lori Jamison Rog ISBN 978-1-55138-303-3

Convince Your Reader

Learning Goal: Students will be able to consider audience and purpose when crafting a piece of persuasive writing.

I DO: Remind students that most of the writing they've been doing recently has been to explain one of their own opinions. As writers, they haven't been too concerned about whether their readers share the same opinion or not. Sometimes, however, writers use I-Think writing to try to persuade their readers to think the same way, and maybe even to take action of some kind.

Share a sample opinion piece such as the one shown here. Discuss with the students the audience and purpose of the piece of writing—the *who* and the *why*. Note that this piece of writing is in the form of a letter to the principal.

WE DO: Together with the students, choose a few topics of interest or concern to many of them. (The list of possible topics on page 89 can be a starting point for your own class chart.) Using the format of the graphic organizer on page 90, talk about *to whom* you might address the concern and *why* they should do something about it. An example is shown below:

Practice orally before asking the students to complete the graphic organizer on their own.

Dear Mr. Persad,
I think we should have longer recess times.

By the time we all get ready to go outside, recess is almost over. And the time is too short to play a whole game of soccer or dodgeball or even Red Rover.

Longer recess would make us healthier because we would get more exercise. Also, we could spend more time outside in the fresh air.

Please think about making our recess times 20 minutes instead of 15 minutes.
Sincerely,
Jadie

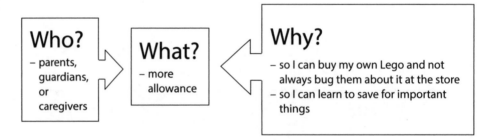

YOU DO: Have students work individually or in pairs to complete the planner on page 90.

Although this minilesson takes the writing only as far as the pre-writing stage, you will probably want to extend it to further minilessons to model completing an I-Think letter to a reader. (This can also be a good opportunity to teach the structure of a letter.) Students also might be given the opportunity to draft, revise, and even publish and send their own persuasive letters.

Ideally, choose a topic that has authentic relevance and concern to your students. Collaborate on crafting a persuasive letter to the principal or to another individual in the school or community.

Things I'd Like to Change

Things at Home

- Bed time
- What we eat
- Pets
- More TV or online time
- Allowance
- Brothers/sisters
- Family vacations

Things in the World

- Smoking
- Recycling
- Holidays and special days
- Movies and video games
- Cell phones
- Healthy living
- Transportation

Things at School

- Longer recess
- More gym
- Less homework
- More play time
- Different food for lunch
- More field trips
- Later school start
- More choice of what we get to study
- More computer/online time

Pembroke Publishers © 2015 *Marvelous Minilessons for Teaching Beginning Nonfiction Writing, K-3* by Lori Jamison Rog ISBN 978-1-55138-303-3

Convince Your Reader Planner

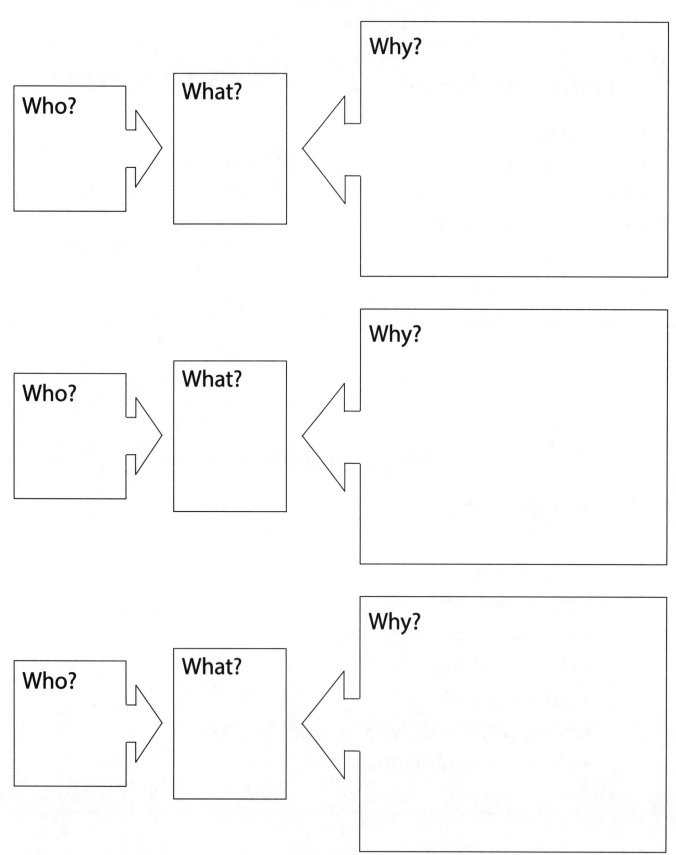

Pembroke Publishers © 2015 *Marvelous Minilessons for Teaching Beginning Nonfiction Writing, K-3* by Lori Jamison Rog ISBN 978-1-55138-303-3

GO-GO Beginnings

Learning Goal: Students will be able to open a piece of persuasive writing with a *grabber* and an *opinion*.

I DO: This lesson has nothing to do with disco dancing! Rather, "GO-GO" is a simple acronym that reminds students to start their I-Think writing with a "grabber" and an opinion. (Note to teachers: You may want to preface this lesson with **"Start with a Grabber"** on page 70.)

Remind students that they already know about what good leads do: they *grab* a reader's attention and make the reader want to read on. *You've already learned to start a piece of I-Think writing by stating your opinion about a topic. And we've talked in the past about grabbing our readers' attention to make them want to read on. So, if you put a "grabber" and an "opinion" together, you have the G-O of "GO-GO Beginnings."*

Revisit a sample of I-Think writing, such as this piece from the minilesson **"What's I-Think Writing?"** (page 81). *When I wrote this I-Think piece, I started with my opinion: We need more books for our classroom library. But maybe there's a better way to grab my reader's attention.* The I-Think piece below is a revision of the sample on page 81, with a GO-GO beginning added.

We Need More Books!

What's the best way to get smarter? Read more! That's why I think we need more books in our classroom library. Most of the students have read most of the books. And not everyone is interested in every book. There just aren't enough books for a whole year. Lots of the books are in bad shape. They've been read over and over again until they're falling apart. It's important for kids to read a lot. So we need to make sure there are a lot of books for them to read.

Discuss other writers' techniques that students know about for grabbing a reader's attention (e.g., start with an amazing fact, as on page 70).

WE DO: Compose together or have students work in pairs to add a GO-GO beginning to another sample text, such as the I-Think letter about longer recess times (see page 88). You might come up with something like: "Healthier kids are better learners. That's why we need to have longer recesses at school."

YOU DO: Ask students to create a GO-GO beginning for one or more of their own drafts of I-Think Writing.

Wraparound Endings

Learning Goal: Students will be able to conclude a piece of I-Think writing by restating their opinion in another way.

I DO: Revisit the OREO organizer to point out that I-Think writing often begins and ends with a statement of the writer's opinion. The opinion "wraps around" the piece at the beginning and at the end.

Of course, our readers might lose interest if the piece of writing says exactly the same thing at the beginning and at the end. If writers want their readers to pay attention, they need to restate their opinion using some of the same words and also some different words. (See also **All-in-All Endings** on page 71.)

Review the I-Think piece about the need for more books for the classroom library (page 81). Note that the writer has "wrapped around" the ending by stating the gist of the opinion again, but using slightly different words. *Which words have been repeated? Which words are different?*

WE DO: Look at another I-Think example together, using the student piece shown here or a sample of your own. Students might work collaboratively to come up with a different way to restate the opinion. (An example might be: "It's time to 'butt out.'") Try two or three alternatives and together select the most effective one.

YOU DO: In Writing Workshop, students should revisit their own I-Think writing pieces to craft wraparound endings that restate the opinion in another way.

It's Time to "Butt Out"!

Puff! Puff! Cough! Cough! Do you know how yucky it is to walk by a person who is smoking? I think grown-ups should stop smoking. You know it is very bad for your health. And it's just as bad for people around you to breathe in the smoke. Smoking costs a lot of money. Wouldn't it be better to spend that money on holidays or food or your kids? It's time for everyone to just stop smoking!

Shouting Sentences

Learning Goal: Students will be able to identify and use exclamatory sentences in opinion/persuasive writing.

I DO: Remind students that a sentence is a special group of words that has a *who* or a *what* and an *is* or a *does*. They already know about some different kinds of sentences; in today's lesson, they will learn about special kinds of sentences that we call "shouting sentences."

Start by reviewing the different kinds of sentences that students already know: "telling" (declarative) sentences, "asking" (interrogative) sentences, and "bossy" (imperative) sentences. Shouting sentences show excitement or strong feelings and we end them with an exclamation mark.

Revisit any of the persuasive text samples in the preceding lessons, such as the piece on more books for the library. Ask students what kinds of sentences they notice. They should be able to find plenty of telling sentences as well as one asking sentence and one shouting sentence.

Shouting sentences should be used just now and then, to add "punch" to the writing. If there are too many shouting sentences, the piece is not effective. In fact, it might seem too angry or even silly to a reader. Imagine a conversation where every sentence was yelling. That sounds more like fighting than persuading! Instead, use one or two shouting sentences to show the reader that these ideas are particularly important.

WE DO: If you think your students need more practice composing shouting sentences, play the question-and-answer game. Ask a question and have students work with partners to come up with an answer that's an exclamation. Take, for example, the question, "What would you like for lunch?" An answer such as "I'd like a tuna sandwich" is a telling sentence, but "I could eat pizza every day!" is a shouting sentence. Some sample questions may be found in the box at the left.

Then have students revise a sample text such as the longer recess piece (page 88) by adding at least one exclamation.

YOU DO: Tell students that in Writing Workshop, they should revise their persuasive writing piece by including at least one question and one exclamation.

You might add a little motivation—and make your on-the-spot assessments easier—by allowing students to highlight their shouting sentence.

Sample Questions to Practice Exclamatory Sentences

- What's your favorite thing to do on the weekend?
- What's something that really bugs you?
- What's the funniest thing you can think of?
- What's something that's not fair?

Four Kinds of Sentences

Telling sentences give information or a message. They end with a period.

Asking sentences ask a question. They end with a question mark.

Bossy sentences give orders. They usually end with a period, but sometimes with an exclamation mark.

Shouting sentences show strong feelings or excitement. They end with an exclamation mark.

Pembroke Publishers © 2015 *Marvelous Minilessons for Teaching Beginning Nonfiction Writing, K-3* by Lori Jamison Rog ISBN 978-1-55138-303-3

The Magic of Three

Learning Goal: Students will be able to use three parallel words or phrases to strengthen the impact of their opinion/persuasive writing.

I DO: Show students a sentence such as the following excerpt from *Angelica Sprocket's Pockets* by Quentin Blake (Jonathan Cape, 2010):

> **"There's a pocket for mice and a pocket for cheese and a pocket for hankies in case you sneeze."**

Invite students to identify Blake's use of three parallel groups of words in the sentence.

There's something about our English language that lends itself to putting words and phrases in groups of three. Using three words or three groups of words together gives our writing a sort of rhythm and makes it sound more musical. When writing sounds smooth to a reader's ear, that reader is more likely to pay attention to the ideas in the writing. Putting words or phrases in groups of three is a writer's trick that we call "The Magic of Three."

WE DO: Have students work in pairs on some oral language practice using "The Magic of Three" technique. You might display missing-word sentences such as the following and have students TTYN (Talk to Your Neighbor) about three words or groups of words to complete each sentence.

We could see _____, _____, and _____ in the night sky.

The dancers were _____, _____, and _____.

_____, _____, and _____ swam past the window of the aquarium.

YOU DO: Revisit a piece of I-Think writing to add at least one example of "The Magic of Three": either a set of three words or three groups of words.

I-Think Writing Rubric

Each level is assumed to also include the criteria from the previous level, even if the criteria are not directly stated.

Level 1	Level 2	Level 3	Level 4
☐ States an opinion and gives at least one good reason	☐ Opens by stating an opinion ☐ Adds "because" with at least two reasons ☐ Includes a shouting sentence	☐ Opens with a GO-GO beginning to grab the reader's attention and state an opinion ☐ Includes at least two reasons ☐ Uses "The Magic of Three" ☐ Includes at least one asking sentence and one shouting sentence ☐ Concludes with a wrap-around ending that restates the opinion	☐ Opens with a GO-GO beginning ☐ Writes to persuade a reader ☐ Includes at least two strong reasons to support the opinion ☐ Offers reasonable explanations for the reasons ☐ Uses "The Magic of Three" to make writing more effective ☐ Includes at least one asking sentence and one shouting sentence ☐ Concludes with a wrap-around ending that restates the opinion

Chapter 6   Putting It All Together: The Multi-Genre Project

Seven-year-old Hayden is obsessed with Lego. He collects Lego, builds with Lego, and even runs a Lego Club. So it was no surprise that he chose Lego as his topic for a Grade 2 writing project. He created an "All-About Lego" report, an I-Think piece on why he believes Lego is the greatest toy of all time, and a procedural piece called "How-To Create Your Own Lego Robot." Motivated by this opportunity to write about his favorite topic, he created a photo journal describing his trip to Legoland, along with captioned pictures and a map.

Under other circumstances, we might tear out our collective hair at the child who cannot get past a single topic; in this case, however, it's a way for kids to see that different text forms can serve different purposes and give different information about the same topic.

Hayden's collection of writing is the start of what we call a "Multi-Genre Project" and it's a terrific way to end a year of studies on different writing genres and text forms. A multi-genre project may appear as a book, a display, a folder, or a digital presentation, but it always incorporates a range of different text forms and text features, all with a common theme.

Even Kindergarteners can participate in multi-genre writing by combining two or three different text forms written on a common topic, although they might need a little more guidance or some graphic organizers in order to expand their range. For example, Rachel created an Are/Have/Can report on birds, a labeled diagram of a peacock, a "Fascinating Facts about Birds" list, and an I-Think piece about why the peacock is her favorite bird.

A multi-genre project is an opportunity to expand students' thinking and to apply their understanding of writing text forms. There is always the expectation that students will include an All-About, an I-Think, and a How-To. But the options for writing in additional text forms are virtually unlimited, from illustrated lists to letters (to real or imaginary readers) to news articles. Students might add a challenge such as riddle books and even board games. You can find a sampling of alternative text forms listed on pages 99–102.

As well, students might be expected to include one or more organizational text elements, such as a Table of Contents, a Glossary, or a brief "About the Author" blurb. And let's not forget visual features, such as bold or colored fonts, illustrations (photographs or hand drawings), and graphics such as charts, tables, or maps. A list of possible text features may be found on page 100, but you and your students are likely to think of many more based on your explorations of published writing.

It's easy to get caught up in the glitz of fun fonts and bright colors, but the foundation of the project must always be the writing. Be sure to encourage students to focus on the facts of the All-About, the supported opinions of the I-Think, and the sequential steps of the How-To first and foremost. These three foundational text forms might be considered compulsory components of the multi-genre project, allowing students to choose the other forms of writing they would like to add. The sophistication of the students will determine the amount of guidance and support they will require.

Because this project would be considered "published" writing, it is expected that upper primary students will revise their work for clarity and power and edit it for conventions. Obviously, the expectations for correct conventions will vary depending on the age and abilities of the students. For example, it's unlikely that Kindergarteners will be expected to correct all their spelling and recopy their work, even for a "final" copy. And even in Grade 3, the last thing we want to do is limit students' creativity to words that they know how to spell. We need to establish a consistent standard of correctness for published work—fully understanding that more complex words and sentences are quite likely to be written with errors. For example, we might choose to accept a "bubble gum writing" (inventive spelling) of *evaporashun*, but expect "book writing" (conventional spelling) of high-frequency words such as *they* or *because*. (For a discussion of the teacher's role related to editing, see page 20.) And may I add that this should be an in-class project. The potential for parent or guardian intervention in any homework project makes the learning value for students uneven at best and minimal at worst.

Unlike the other chapters in this book, which contain writing strategy minilessons, this chapter offers ideas and suggestions for products and presentations. You will have to make the call about how you model or teach them.

As the multi-genre project unfolds, your students will be justifiably proud of what they've achieved in writing this year and an end-of-year Author Party is a great way to celebrate.

Writing Celebration (Author Party)

The multi-genre project affords so many opportunities for choice, ownership, and independence that it is sure to engage even the most reluctant writer. All that remains is a celebration of their accomplishments. There are many different ways to organize a writing celebration. Here's one successful format that involves minimum preparation on the teacher's part and maximum attention paid to every student.

Guests for an Author Party may include other students (especially from an older grade), parents or guardians and other family members, the principal or other school (or district) personnel, and perhaps community members. Each student sits at a table or a desk on which his or her project is displayed along with a package of tiny stickers. Place an extra chair for a guest beside each student's display.

When guests arrive, they are given a simple mock "passport" with each student's name in it. They look for any student who has an empty chair beside his or her desk and they sit down to listen to the student read some (his or her choice) of the writing on display. After the reading, the guest compliments the student on the project and the student "stamps" the guest's passport by putting a small sticker beside his or her own name. Then the guest moves on to another student who has an empty chair and the process continues.

Ideally, this event might last no more than 30 minutes. Every student will have an opportunity to share his or her project with several guests and hear compliments about the work that was shared. This interaction with guest readers is a wonderful boost for the child's image as a writer and provides an authentic audience for writing.

Tips for a Successful Author Party

Additional tips to ensure that an Author Party is a success include the following:

- Make sure students have practiced reading *all* their writing pieces so they can read fluently and expressively for their audience.
- You may wish to spend a little time preparing students for the social niceties of greeting a guest, accepting compliments, and saying good-bye and thank you.
- Invite more guests than students, so that no student is ever sitting and waiting for someone to come to sit beside him or her.
- Have some snacks on hand for guests to enjoy as they wait for an available student to visit.
- On a program or on a poster displayed in the classroom, offer suggestions for the kinds of comments guests might offer the students, for example:
    I liked the part where...
    The fact that surprised me most was...
    I loved the way you said...
    A terrific word you used was...
    This part was so interesting because...
    You sounded like a real author when...

Ten Ideas for Other Writing Formats

There's no limit to the forms and features of writing that are appropriate for a multi-genre project. The following ten suggestions are just a starting point; you and your students are likely to come up with many more. Any text forms that students are *required* to apply should be explicitly taught and practiced. Some suggested templates and graphic organizers are included at the end of this chapter. More sophisticated writers probably won't need a template, but the organizers might be useful for Kindergarteners and others who need additional support.

- **Illustrated List**
This writing format is especially appropriate for Kindergarteners, but it may be used effectively by students at all ages and stages. It's often a good format for including the "other interesting facts" on a topic that may not fit anywhere else in the report. The list doesn't really need to be illustrated if the writer chooses to use only words. A template for an illustrated list can be found on page 105. The flapbook template (page 102) offers an engaging alternative to an illustrated list.

Multi-Genre Project Organizer

_____'s WRITING PROJECT

TOPIC: _____

_____

☐ All-About _____

☐ How-To _____

☐ I-Think _____

At least three other writing pieces:

1. _____

2. _____

3. _____

Text Organizers

☐ Table of Contents   ☐ Chart

☐ About the Author   ☐ Graph

☐ Glossary   ☐ Close-up

☐ Where I Got My Information   ☐ Cross-section

☐ Index   ☐ Fancy Fonts and Colors

Text Features

☐ Illustration with caption

☐ Labeled diagram

☐ Map

Pembroke Publishers © 2015 *Marvelous Minilessons for Teaching Beginning Nonfiction Writing, K-3* by Lori Jamison Rog ISBN 978-1-55138-303-3

- **Letters**

There are many ways that letters may be used as part of a multi-genre project. In Chapter 5, we looked at ways to write a persuasive letter. Letters may be written to or from imaginary or real-life readers. Hayden's project on Lego might include, for example, a letter to Ole Kirk Christiansen, the inventor of Lego; a letter to a friend describing or explaining a new Lego creation; or a letter to his teacher persuading her to create a Lego blocks learning centre. Postcards are an informal type of letter featuring a picture on one side and a hand-written message on the other.

- **ABC Book**

An alphabet book is another variation on the illustrated list; it provides a reader-friendly organizer for information that is not necessarily presented topically. However, the task of writing 26 pages or even 26 facts is likely to prove onerous for many young writers; as well, trying to find a fact for every letter (especially x, y, and z!) might result in contrived or insignificant facts rather than the most relevant ones. Therefore, I suggest that students choose only a limited number of letters when composing an ABC book. An "acrostic poem" uses the letters in the name of a topic as the initial letter of each line. (See the example on the left.)

- **Poem**

Many students might have fun with rhyming couplets that present facts on a topic, such as: "The hippo is truly a dangerous creature/His terrible breath is one scary feature." Of course, not all poetry needs to rhyme; information about a topic may be effectively conveyed in free verse as well. If you've taught the poetry genre in your writing program, you might request a poem as one of the text forms in the students' multi-genre project. "Tree poems" may not fulfill many criteria for high-quality poetry but they are unique and interesting text forms for conveying information. Each line has one more word than the previous line, ultimately resulting in a pyramid or tree shape. A template for writing a tree poem appears on page 106.

- **News Report**

What is newsworthy about your topic? Hayden was fascinated by the story of a house built entirely of Lego—including the toilet! A little research could lead to a *who, what, when, where, why,* and *how* story worthy of the daily news. There are many news report templates available online, and a simple one is included on page 107.

- **Games and Riddles**

What's more fun than a little friendly competition? A board game or even a card game can be an effective tool for conveying information on a topic. Players might move a marker along the board by answering questions about the topic. A snakes-and-ladders type of format adds an element of chance. One challenge related to this format is not only to convey information about the topic, but also to establish viable rules for the game.

- **Q & A**

Questions and answers (or answers and questions, as in the television show "Jeopardy") are another way to convey random facts about a topic. Students could create flash cards, with questions on one side and answers on the other. Another option is to create a flap book (see instructions on page 102).

- **Poster**

A poster itself may be multi-genre, if it consists of a combination of print, visuals, and even glued-on artifacts to convey information about a topic. You may wish to teach students how to organize a poster effectively using elements such as an overall title and captions for visuals.

- **Interview with an Expert**

Internet and print materials aren't the only sources of information about a topic. A sit-down, telephone, or Skype interview with an expert can yield a lot of useful information. (And an "expert" doesn't have to be a stranger; it could be a parent, grandparent, teacher, or another student.) Interviewing also teaches students about asking good questions and recording answers carefully. Students should restrict their questions to no more than four or five and they should submit their questions to their teacher for approval prior to conducting the interview, which must take place in a safe setting with a parent or other responsible adult present.

- **Slide Show or Photo Journal**

Students can produce a collection of pictures with captions in the form of a slide show in digital format, or in the form of a photo journal. Pictures may be hand drawn, but in these types of formats, photographs are usually more effective.

Foldables and Pop-ups

Foldables are simply graphic organizers that students can create by folding a sheet of paper (rather than your having to stand in line for the photocopier). Instructions for making lift-the-flap books are found below.

Pop-ups add a fun three-dimensional component to any piece of writing. Check out the following website to see how to create a terrific illustrated How-To pop-up from author Robert Sabuda: http://wp.robertsabuda.com/How-To-make-a-pop-up-layer/

Lift-the-Flap Book

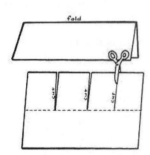

Lift-the-flap books can have as many flaps as you choose. This sample uses four flaps, which are easy to fold.

1. Fold a piece of paper in half lengthwise (hotdog fold).
2. Then fold it in half crosswise (hamburger fold) twice, so that the paper is folded in eight.

Unfold the paper. Along the top half, cut along each vertical fold line only to the centre fold, so that the bottom is one solid piece and the top consists of four flaps.

Fold the page over again so that the flaps are on top and the solid piece is underneath. The lift-the-flap book can be used horizontally or vertically.

About the Author

○

_____ is _____

_____

_____

_____

_____

_____ chose this topic because _____

_____

_____

An important thing _____ learned was

_____

_____

Pembroke Publishers © 2015 *Marvelous Minilessons for Teaching Beginning Nonfiction Writing, K-3* by Lori Jamison Rog ISBN 978-1-55138-303-3

Table of Contents

Topics or Chapters   Page

_____

_____

_____

_____

_____

_____

_____

_____

_____

_____

_____

_____

_____

_____

_____

Pembroke Publishers © 2015 *Marvelous Minilessons for Teaching Beginning Nonfiction Writing, K-3* by Lori Jamison Rog ISBN 978-1-55138-303-3

Fascinating Facts About

_____

_____

_____

_____

_____

_____

_____

_____

_____

_____

Tree Poem

THE DAILY NEWS

_____

```
┌─────────────────────┐          _____
│                     │
│                     │          _____
│                     │
│                     │          _____
│                     │
│                     │          _____
│                     │
│                     │          _____
└─────────────────────┘
```

_____

_____

_____

_____

_____

_____

_____

_____

_____

_____

Pembroke Publishers © 2015 *Marvelous Minilessons for Teaching Beginning Nonfiction Writing, K-3* by Lori Jamison Rog ISBN 978-1-55138-303-3

Where I Got My Information

BOOKS and MAGAZINES

Title: _____

Author: _____   Book's Birthday: _____

Title: _____

Author: _____   Book's Birthday: _____

WEBSITES

Name: _____

Web Address (URL): _____

EXPERTS

Name: _____

Interview Date: _____

Person's Role or Job Title: _____

Resources

Calkins, L. (1983). *Lessons from a Child.* New York: Portsmouth NH: Heinemann.

Clarke, L. K. (1988). Invented versus traditional spelling in first graders' writings: Effects on learning to spell and read. *Research in the Teaching of English,* 22, 281-309.

College Board. (2003). *The Neglected "R": A Need for a Writing Revolution.* The National Commission on Writing in America's Schools and Colleges.

Cutler, Laura & Graham, Steve. (2008). Primary grade writing instruction: A national survey, *Journal of Educational Psychology,* 100:4, 907-919.

Graham, S. & Perrin, D. (2007). *Writing Next: Effective Strategies to Improve Writing of Adolescents in Middle and High School.* New York: Carnegie Corporation of New York.

Hidi, S. & Anderson, V. (2014). Situational interest and its impact on reading and expository writing. In Renninger, K.A., Hidi, S. & Krapp (Eds), *The Role of Interest in Learning and Development.* New York, NY: Psychology Press, 217.

Jacobson, J. (2010). *No More "I'm Done!"* Portland, ME: Stenhouse.

Jamison, Rog, L. (2006). *Marvelous Minilessons for Teaching Beginning Writing K-3.* Newark, DE: International Reading Association.

Jamison, Rog, L. (2010). *Marvelous Minilessons for Teaching Intermediate Writing, Grades 4-6.* Newark, DE: International Reading Association.

Kohn, A. (September 1993). Choices for children: Why and how to let students decide. *Phi Delta Kappan;* http://www.alfiekohn.org/article/choices-children/; downloaded 16/10/2015.

Children's Literature Cited

Blake, Q. (2010). *Angelica Sprocket's Pockets.* Jonathan Cape.

Brown, L. (2006). *How to Be.* HarperCollins.

Burningham, J. (1994). *Would You Rather?* Red Fox.

Cronin, D. (2013). *Diary of a Spider.* HarperCollins.

Davies, N. (1997). *Big Blue Whale.* Candlewick.

Reagan, J. (2012). *How to Babysit a Grandpa.* Knopf.

Rosenthal, A. K. (2009). *Duck! Rabbit!* Chronicle Books.

Shores, E. (2011). *How to Make Bubbles.* Capstone Press.

Silverstein, S. (1974). *Where the Sidewalk Ends.* Harper & Row.

Watt, M. (2011). *Scaredy Squirrel Makes a Friend.* Kids Can Press.

Index